Beloved Enos

By

Denver C. Snuffer, Jr.

Mill Creek Press
Salt Lake City, Utah

Published in the United States by Mill Creek Press.

MILL CREEK PRESS is a registered trademark of
Mill Creek Press, LLC

Library of Congress Control Number 2009900752

ISBN: 978-0-9798455-8-1

Printed in the United States of America on acid-free paper
Mill Creek Press website address: www.millcreekpress.com
pfb32975

First Edition

Take my yoke upon you, and learn of me; for I am meek and lowly in heart: and ye shall find rest unto your souls.
(Matt. 11: 29.)

Table of Contents

SUMMARY OF ABBREVIATIONS USED:

The following abbreviations will be used for the authorities frequently cited in this work:

History of the Church of Jesus Christ of Latter-day Saints, 7 Volumes, published by the Church of Jesus Christ of Latter-day Saints; will be cited as *"DHC"* followed by volume number and page (i.e., *DHC* 6: 23).

Teachings of the Prophet Joseph Smith, arranged by Joseph Fielding Smith, published by Deseret Book Company; will be cited as *"TPJS"* followed by the page number (i.e., *TPJS* p. 23).

The Words of Joseph Smith, compiled by Andrew F. Ehat and Lyndon W. Cook, published by the Religious Studies Center, Brigham Young University; will be cited as *"WJS"* followed by the page number (i.e., *WJS* p. 23).

The Journal of Discourses, 26 volumes, will be cited as *"JD"* followed by the volume and page number (i.e., *JD* 6: 23).

Lectures on Faith, compiled by N.B. Lundwall, published by Bookcraft; will be cited as *"Lectures"* followed by Lecture Number and paragraph (i.e., *Lectures,* 4: 90-91).

The Second Comforter: Conversing With the Lord Through the Veil, Denver C. Snuffer, Jr., published by Mill Creek Press, Salt Lake City, 2006; will be cited as *The Second Comforter*.

Nephi's Isaiah, Denver C. Snuffer, Jr., published by Mill Creek Press, Salt Lake City, 2006; will be cited as *Nephi's Isaiah*.

References to the Bible are to the King James Version.

All other authorities are cited at length.

All spellings in quotes have been left as in the original. To prevent the frequent repetition of "[sic]" we take note of that here, and will not otherwise acknowledge antiquated spellings within the text.

PREFACE:

Enos is a delightful but challenging writer. He is singular in his ability to write scripture using sacred symbols. He condenses his materials into powerful, but cryptic content. He is best understood by parsing his words carefully to notice the many symbols and their meanings.

Enos may very well be one of the most intelligent composers of scripture in history. He certainly stands out in the Book of Mormon. His life brought him into contact with God, and his book makes careful use of symbols to communicate to the latter-day readers about these sacred events. He is a mystic, a prophet, a composer of prose, acquainted with deep doctrine and adept at putting it into words.

We are going to look at the words used in the book to reconstruct the larger picture of sacred events from Enos' life. What will emerge is both delightful and astonishing. We have given too little time to Enos in our Book of Mormon studies. I hope to identify him as one of the greatest prophets of history. His book may be short in word count, but it is certainly towering in content.

The material Enos covers is most sacred. When the scriptures force us to encounter and recognize sacred matters we need to be equal to the task. As long as we accept holy matters with respect and devotion there is no reason to shy away from discussing them. Unless we search into sacred matters we will never understand the scriptures. As Jacob put it: "Wherefore, we search the prophets, and we have many revelations and the spirit of prophecy; and having all these witnesses we obtain a hope, and our faith becometh unshaken, insomuch that we truly can command in the name of Jesus and the very trees obey us, or the mountains, or the waves of the sea." (Jacob 4: 6.) Enos was Jacob's son. He wrote about searching, revelation and the spirit of prophecy. Therefore when we discuss Enos we must encounter these very sacred topics. Joseph Smith taught: "I advise all to go on to perfection, and search deeper and deeper into the mysteries of Godliness." (*TPJS*, p. 364.) We need to understand Enos if we are going to search deeper and deeper into the mysteries of Godliness.

This book covers some of the same material I have taught in a Book of Mormon class. It has been written to make the concepts taught available to a wider audience. Some concepts are not well defined in existing books. The Gospel restored to us is so interesting, inviting, stimulating and interesting it should keep our interest. If you are bored it is because you have not yet found what you are looking for. There is no more vast a subject than the Gospel of Jesus Christ. I hope this book will stimulate your curiosity about it, and inspire your devotion to it.

The interpretation given in this book is not the only way to view Enos' writing. It is offered as just one way to understand this important Book of Mormon writer.

I want to thank my wife, Stephanie, for suggesting I write this book and for providing editing. I also want to thank Mill Creek Press for continuing to support my writing. I hope this will prove a valuable source for all who would like to learn to carefully interpret all of the words in the text of the Book of Mormon. The approach used here with Enos can be used in reading the entire text.

This is the product of one person's thinking. The book is not approved or sponsored by anyone and the author alone is responsible for its contents. If, however, credit be due to anyone for this book, then it is due to the Lord who alone is the author of all truth. The author has merely repeated in his weakness what the Lord can provide to anyone in His strength.

Denver C. Snuffer, Jr.
March 1, 2009
Sandy, Utah

Beloved Enos

Chapter 1

INTRODUCTION

$\mathcal{A}$s an attorney I struggle with questions of proof and persuasion every day of my professional life. The law requires facts to be proven, but the standard of proof required varies depending upon the kind of case involved. For civil matters involving contract or tort claims, proof is required by a preponderance of the evidence. Such questions are resolved by it appearing more likely than not that a fact is true. Fraud claims must be proven by clear and convincing proof. Criminal cases require proof beyond any reasonable doubt before a conviction. When approaching any case a lawyer must always consider the standard of proof required and determine whether the evidence gathered for the case can meet the applicable standard. Interestingly, there are three levels of proof that get applied in the law.

Religious proof is another matter altogether. No matter how persuasive an argument may be for or against a religious proposition, such a question can never be decided by relying on another's proof alone. Argument, evidence and sincerity have led people to opposite conclusions throughout history. Religious conviction was used as the reason for both following Christ as well as killing Him. Religious wars are frequent and show no signs of diminishing.

One of Joseph Smith's brilliant insights came as a youth, in his fifteenth year according to his recollection. (See JS-H 1: 7.) He determined that religious confusion needed to be resolved between the individual and God. He retells it with these words, "I was one day reading the Epistle of James, first chapter and fifth verse, which reads: If any of you lack wisdom, let him ask of God, that giveth to all men liberally, and upbraideth not; and it shall be given him. Never did any passage of scripture come with more power to the heart of man than this did at this time to mine. It seemed to enter with great force into every feeling of my heart. I reflected on it again and again, knowing that if any person needed wisdom from God, I did; for how to act I did not know, and unless I could get more wisdom than I then had, I would never know; for the teachers of religion of the different sects understood the same passages of scripture so differently as to destroy all confidence in settling the question by an appeal to the Bible. At length I came to the conclusion that I must either remain in darkness and confusion, or else I must do as James directs, that is, ask of God. I at length came to the determination to 'ask of God,' concluding that if he gave wisdom to them that lacked wisdom, and would give liberally, and not upbraid, I might venture." (JS-H 1: 11-13.) In accordance with that determination Joseph asked. God answered. When God answered we had a modern day confirmation from an eye-witness of how this should work.

Oddly, the focus on what Joseph Smith accomplished takes attention away from the fundamental lesson for which Joseph stands. His personal experience has wrongly become the focus. But what he says he saw, heard or learned is not the real issue at all. His experience can be debated, his credibility can be challenged, his competence can be argued, even his sanity can be questioned, but that is all beside the point. Joseph set an example to be *followed*, not debated. If God spoke to Joseph, then all Joseph really stands for is the proposition that God will speak to anyone who lacks wisdom and asks. Joseph is telling us he trusted James. If there is an individual whose credibility is in question and whose word is being tested, it is James and not Joseph. It all comes down to you. You are supposed to gather your own proof by asking God yourself. The level of proof which God provides is clearly a sliding scale. It begins with belief enough to support an experiment in which you try to follow God. This process is described in Alma 32: 27-43.[1] The scale

[1]"But behold, if ye will awake and arouse your faculties, even to an experiment upon my words, and exercise a particle of faith, yea, even if ye can no more than desire to believe, let this desire work in you, even until ye believe in a manner that ye can give place for a portion of my words. Now, we will compare the word unto a seed. Now, if ye give place, that a seed may be planted in your heart, behold, if it be a true seed, or a good seed, if ye do not cast it out by your unbelief, that ye will resist the Spirit of the Lord, behold, it will begin to swell within your breasts; and when you feel these swelling motions, ye will begin to say within yourselves--It must needs be that this is a good seed, or that the word is good, for it beginneth to enlarge my soul; yea, it beginneth to enlighten my understanding, yea, it beginneth to be delicious to me. Now behold, would not this increase your faith? I say unto you, Yea; nevertheless it hath not grown up to a perfect knowledge. But behold, as the seed swelleth, and sprouteth, and beginneth to grow, then you must needs say that the seed is good; for behold it swelleth, and sprouteth, and beginneth to grow. And now, behold, will not this strengthen your faith? Yea, it will strengthen your faith: for ye will say I know that this is a good seed; for behold it sprouteth and beginneth to grow. And now, behold, are ye sure that this is a good seed? I say unto you, Yea; for every seed bringeth forth unto its own likeness. Therefore, if a seed groweth it is good, but if it groweth not, behold it is not good, therefore it is cast away. And now, behold, because ye have tried the experiment, and planted the seed, and it swelleth and sprouteth, and beginneth to grow, ye must needs know that the seed is good. And now, behold, is your knowledge perfect? Yea, your knowledge is perfect in that thing, and your faith is dormant; and this because you know, for ye know that the word hath swelled your souls,

concludes at the other end with positive knowledge gained by a personal visit from the Second Comforter, or Jesus Christ. As revealed to Joseph: "Verily, thus saith the Lord: It shall come to pass that every soul who forsaketh his sins and cometh unto me, and calleth on my name, and obeyeth my voice, and keepeth my commandments, shall see my face and know that I am." (D&C 93: 1.) You and I are allowed to gather such proof from God as we want; from a mere preponderance to beyond any reasonable doubt.

---

and ye also know that it hath sprouted up, that your understanding doth begin to be enlightened, and your mind doth begin to expand. O then, is not this real? I say unto you, Yea, because it is light; and whatsoever is light, is good, because it is discernible, therefore ye must know that it is good; and now behold, after ye have tasted this light is your knowledge perfect? Behold I say unto you, Nay; neither must ye lay aside your faith, for ye have only exercised your faith to plant the seed that ye might try the experiment to know if the seed was good. And behold, as the tree beginneth to grow, ye will say: Let us nourish it with great care, that it may get root, that it may grow up, and bring forth fruit unto us. And now behold, if ye nourish it with much care it will get root, and grow up, and bring forth fruit. But if ye neglect the tree, and take no thought for its nourishment, behold it will not get any root; and when the heat of the sun cometh and scorcheth it, because it hath no root it withers away, and ye pluck it up and cast it out. Now, this is not because the seed was not good, neither is it because the fruit thereof would not be desirable; but it is because your ground is barren, and ye will not nourish the tree, therefore ye cannot have the fruit thereof. And thus, if ye will not nourish the word, looking forward with an eye of faith to the fruit thereof, ye can never pluck of the fruit of the tree of life. But if ye will nourish the word, yea, nourish the tree as it beginneth to grow, by your faith with great diligence, and with patience, looking forward to the fruit thereof, it shall take root; and behold it shall be a tree springing up unto everlasting life. And because of your diligence and your faith and your patience with the word in nourishing it, that it may take root in you, behold, by and by ye shall pluck the fruit thereof, which is most precious, which is sweet above all that is sweet, and which is white above all that is white, yea, and pure above all that is pure; and ye shall feast upon this fruit even until ye are filled, that ye hunger not, neither shall ye thirst. Then, my brethren, ye shall reap the rewards of your faith, and your diligence, and patience, and long-suffering, waiting for the tree to bring forth fruit unto you."

It is left to each of us to decide, by our heed and diligence, what level of light we will attain to in this life. Whatever degree of light we accept here will follow us into the next life. (See D&C 130: 18-19.) We attain the level of proof we want by asking God to answer our questions. And, as Joseph reminded us, God does not upbraid (or scold) the asker. God gives liberally. Some people have such positive experiences from contact with God that they have knowledge beyond any doubts. (See e.g., Ether 3: 19-20.)

Joseph has not been the one on trial from the time of his reported First Vision. It has instead been each of us. We don't need to accept Joseph's word on anything because the thought which activated Joseph's faith came from James. Both James and Joseph assure us that God speaks. From that bit of information we all go on trial. Do we ask? Do we trust God will answer? Do we seek for light and truth? Are we willing to accept the challenge and seek guidance for ourselves from God? Can we also duplicate Joseph's experience and go through the process of getting answers for ourselves from God? Those are questions for us to answer, not Joseph.

Joseph can be a naive, money-grubbing, backwoods farm boy. He can be as insecure as any poorly educated man would be if noticed by the world. It does not affect the question of whether we can obtain personal guidance from God. It is clear beyond dispute that such flaws appear in many of the Biblical prophets. Some of the "Lord's anointed" prophets from bygone days are not the sort any of us would want to invite to dinner. Sampson's life was a mess, his spiritual and physical endowments being a curse rather than a blessing. David was fatally lustful and willing to murder to conceal his sins. Peter was overly impulsive, blurting out instead of reflecting before speaking. Hosea's wife had been a prostitute (imagine how a typical LDS ward may have viewed them). Jonah was vindictive and reluctant. Lot inexplicably lived in Sodom until Abraham came and took him from the place. Aaron made a golden-calf idol at the behest of the foolish. We have a frail and human assortment of men in the Biblical record whose many failings are at least equal to any claimed to be Joseph's. Even Joseph's "scandalous" introduction of multiple wives pales in comparison to the Patriarchs. If Joseph had as many as 36 multiple wives (as some reckon) he was an underachiever by comparison to David's 1,000 wives and concubines and Solomon' greater number still. Joseph's modest accomplishment in producing progeny makes Abraham[2] and Jacob/Isaac look virile by comparison.

It isn't Joseph we need to be concerned with. It is the God of Heaven who spoke to Joseph who is the real issue. First, we should resolve the issue of whether God CAN still speak to mankind. If so, then will He speak to you? Joseph stands for the proposition that one recently lived life enjoyed God's direct involvement. It opens the possibility God can continue to be involved with any life. But the proof of God's involvement remains to be demonstrated in your own life. If you don't hear from Him then Joseph's contact is largely meaningless. Joseph taught that promises made to anyone else are unrelated to you. You must go get your own.[3]

---

[2]Abraham's progeny include the often overlooked children he sired with Keturah. (See Gen. 25: 1-4.)

[3]"You, no doubt, will agree with us, and say, that you have no right to claim the promises of the inhabitants before the flood; that you cannot found your hopes of salvation upon the obedience of the children of Israel when journeying in the wilderness, nor can you expect that the blessings which the apostles pronounced upon the churches of Christ eighteen hundred years ago, were intended for you. Again, if others' blessings are not your blessings, others' curses are not your curses; you stand then in these last days, as all have stood before you, agents unto

I, too, have asked questions of God. To my great joy, God has spoken to me. I have proof satisfactory enough for my own convictions. As a result, I am satisfied Joseph was able to get answers from God and what Joseph recorded from his experiences is important for me to study. This is not because Joseph is a man upon whom I place any reliance, but because God has satisfied me that He did speak to Joseph. As a result, it is God in whom I place my trust, not Joseph. Joseph was His tool, but God is the craftsman who fashioned a restoration of His Gospel using a flawed, human prophet. Joseph's flaws are interesting, even consoling to me. They do not discourage my faith in God.

I accept as true that Joseph Smith was a prophet of God. I trust he was enlightened by God in sacred knowledge which relates to the structure of the universe. I expect Joseph was given by the Lord firsthand, the same kind of knowledge which is promised to be revealed by the Lord to all others when He appears for all mankind to see. I believe Joseph received as part of his calling as a prophet, the knowledge described in revelation as follows: "Yea, verily I say unto you, in that day when the Lord shall come, he shall reveal all things--Things which have passed, and hidden things which no man knew, things of the earth, by which it was made, and the purpose and the end thereof--Things most precious, things that are above, and things that are beneath, things that are in the earth, and upon the earth, and in heaven." (D&C 101: 32-34.)

From those premises I proceed with confidence to the conviction Joseph has great things to share with me. I am both curious and eager to extract what I might from this most recent recipient of a Dispensation of the Gospel of Jesus Christ. I believe the Lord will require that I first acquaint myself with Joseph's

yourselves, to be judged according to your works." (*TPJS* p. 12.)

revelations before I can expect further knowledge revealed directly to me by the same Lord who "giveth liberally to all men, and upbraideth not." (James 1: 5.)

When I compare the **speculation** of scholars, to what Joseph had **revealed** to him, I believe it safe to invariably trust Joseph whenever the two differ. I trust Joseph's certification of the Book of Mormon when he said: "I told the brethren that the Book of Mormon was the most correct of any book on earth, and the keystone of our religion, and a man would get nearer to God by abiding by its precepts, than by any other book." (DHC 4: 461.) I would like to be nearer to God.

Isaiah prophesied of a sealed book which would be able to communicate a vision of all truth. He wrote: "And the vision of all is become unto you as the words of a book that is sealed, which men deliver to one that is learned, saying, Read this, I pray thee: and he saith, I cannot; for it is sealed." (Isa. 29: 11.) I trust the "vision of all" does exist within the Book of Mormon. To the extent I do not see it there I think it is my shortcoming as a reader and not any shortcoming in the content of the book. I would like to understand the vision of all.

I seek constantly to use the Book of Mormon as a tool to move my understanding upward. I would like to have my meditation informed by passages from that book and to exhaust its contents of meaning. To the extent I succeed in taking the Book of Mormon seriously, I believe it incumbent upon the Lord to remove from me any condemnation resting upon mankind because of disrespect of the Book of Mormon,[4] and provide further light and knowledge by

---

[4]D&C 84: 54-57: "And your minds in times past have been darkened because of unbelief, and because you have treated lightly the things you have received--Which vanity and unbelief have brought the whole church under condemnation. And this condemnation resteth upon

revelation, as promised in Alma 12: 9-10.

In addition to the Book of Mormon, I think Joseph's life is also important to study and understand. Richard L. Bushman presented a paper at the Bicentennial Conference at the Library of Congress titled *Joseph Smith's Many Histories*. He asserted, ". . . our histories are detachable. Every nation, every institution, every person can be extricated from one history and attached to another, often with perfect plausibility. Each of us has many histories. The histories I refer to are not the events of our lives, but the various cultural contexts that produce us and explain who we are—our many different pasts." (*The Worlds of Joseph Smith*. Edited by John W. Welch. Provo: Brigham Young University Press, 2006, p. 3.) I can agree with Brother Bushman's point. But the detachable histories written of Joseph, including Brother Bushman's, have failed to provide an adequate basis for using Joseph's ministry for my personal enlightenment. Such scholars' histories may be "true" in every sense, but they do not provide me light from which to advance closer to God using Joseph's teachings as a launching point for my own trip to that "exceedingly high mountain" where men, angels and the Gods may mingle.[5]

---

the children of Zion, even all. And they shall remain under this condemnation until they repent and remember the new covenant, even the Book of Mormon and the former commandments which I have given them, not only to say, but to do according to that which I have written."

[5]See e.g., 1 Ne. 11: 1: "For it came to pass after I had desired to know the things that my father had seen, and believing that the Lord was able to make them known unto me, as I sat pondering in mine heart I was caught away in the Spirit of the Lord, yea, into an exceedingly high mountain, which I never had before seen, and upon which I never had before set my foot." Also Moses 1: 1: "The words of God, which he spake unto Moses at a time when Moses was caught up into an exceedingly high mountain."

I wrote in *The Second Comforter* the following:

> Quinn's work *Early Mormonism and the Magic World
> View* is a study of the cultural setting in which
> Joseph Smith lived. While Quinn correctly
> identifies the setting and the features of the mind
> which developed within that setting, he misses the
> point. Quinn uses our standards to judge Joseph
> Smith's day and time, instead of reversing the
> comparison. We are not superior. Joseph is the one
> who got visions and witnessed angels. We should
> be trying to recapture that kind of a mind, not
> condescending toward it as Quinn and Palmer
> have done. Until we have similar visitations,
> visions and experiences we stand on lower ground.
> To use the lower ground to judge the higher is
> wrongheaded. We should be studying them and
> their time with a bit more humility, rather than just
> assuming we hold the best vantage point from
> which to judge all others. I do not quibble over
> Quinn's accounts of Joseph's time and setting. I
> reject, however, his conclusions. (*The Second
> Comforter*, p. 351-2.)

Joseph made no apologies for his varied spiritual experiences. While
D. Michael Quinn and Grant Palmer have looked with some
skepticism at Joseph's apparently primitive view, I have suggested
this is a flaw in their viewpoint, not Joseph's. In footnote 203 in the
2nd Edition of *The Second Comforter*, I suggest this issue is "worthy of
some treatment in its own right." (*Id.*, p. 243.) I will take up that
point in this book as part of the discussion of Enos' record.

The history of revealed truth, like all other things in this world,
is riddled with entropy. When truth is given to mankind, he

struggles to preserve it; to keep it intact and avoid introducing errors. Our generation cannot be any different. These persistent human tendencies did not suddenly come to an end in 1830. Some of what Joseph Smith restored has lain fallow on the ground, untended by our efforts to produce fruit from his vision.

Joseph Smith was not just a restorer of Primitive Christianity. He was also a restorer of more ancient forms of truth which date back to the dawn of man. As he mentions in passing in his letter now found in Section 128, his visitors included "divers angels, from Michael or Adam down to the present time." (D&C 128: 21.) There is a strong cultural and scholarly effort to confine Joseph to the tidy role of a "Christian" prophet. He may have been a "Christian" prophet, but that is truly a minimalist view of what he accomplished. By the time it had descended to Joseph's day, "Christianity" itself was only a limited echo of what Christ originally brought to mankind.

Joseph thought it possible to know the truth of all things.[6] His

---

[6]See e.g., among other statements the following: Moro 10: 5: "And by the power of the Holy Ghost ye may know the truth of all things." D&C 50: 40: "Behold, ye are little children and ye cannot bear all things now; ye must grow in grace and in the knowledge of the truth." D&C 88: 40: "For intelligence cleaveth unto intelligence; wisdom receiveth wisdom; truth embraceth truth; virtue loveth virtue; light cleaveth unto light; mercy hath compassion on mercy and claimeth her own; justice continueth its course and claimeth its own; judgment goeth before the face of him who sitteth upon the throne and governeth and executeth all things." D&C 93: 28: "He that keepeth his commandments receiveth truth and light, until he is glorified in truth and knoweth all things." D&C 124: 97: "Let my servant William Law also receive the keys by which he may ask and receive blessings; let him be humble before me, and be without guile, and he shall receive of my Spirit, even the

quest was not only to acquire knowledge of the truth for himself but to extend an invitation to all who heard him; go and personally do likewise. He envisioned a peculiar people who were in direct covenant relationship with God; prophets and prophetesses, kings and priests, queens and priestesses, who were worthy of associations with the immortals. He restored what some consider arcane ritual-making, imitative of Masonry or some other cultic practice. His contemporary critics believed him a crackpot. Now some modern scholarly critics consider him a genius and innovator. The critics will never gain the benefits Joseph bequeathed to mankind. Joseph's restoration of covenant making and authoritative ordinances will never bless them. They will never follow the profound patterns for engaging in a dialogue with God which Joseph taught. Unfortunately, neither will most of those who claim to accept Joseph as a prophet.

This book will attempt to explore my own view of how profound a personal ministry Joseph fulfilled. It focuses on the Book of Mormon because I accept it as the most correct book and trust that I can get nearer to God through its precepts than from any other book.

Joseph restored a church organization. However, he never limited the knowledge of truth to that organization. With the Lord's direction and approval, he installed offices and delegated keys given to him so the Church of Jesus Christ could continue to function

---

Comforter, which shall manifest unto him the truth of all things, and shall give him, in the very hour, what he shall say."

authoritatively after Joseph's death. Those keys remain intact and the ordinances of The Church of Jesus Christ of Latter-day Saints are indispensable for salvation. But truth can be found everywhere. It echoes all about us in traditions handed down in every culture, language and people. Some of the great body of revelation restored through Joseph will resonate with cultures that have yet to be converted to the Gospel of Jesus Christ. When they do convert, they will bring with them the ability to see within our scriptures that which eludes us. We wrongly presume we can see past our cultural blinders. We need Buddhists, Muslims and Hindus to come into the family of faith and to bring with them their sensitivity to truths belonging to their faiths. They will see many things in the Standard Works which we cannot.

It is ill-advised for Latter-day Saints to pretend to be part of the "Christian" tradition. The faith restored by Joseph was necessary to come again because the Lord was disgusted with the Historic Christian tradition as it existed in 1820. Its creeds were an abomination. The people who professed all of the various Historic Christian faiths were corrupted by their inadequate understanding of the faith taught by Christ.[7] For us to try to be accepted by such a group, pretending we have nothing further to offer and seeking praise and popular acceptance from other Christian faiths is both a

---

[7]See JS-H 1: 19: "I was answered that I must join none of them, for they were all wrong; and the Personage who addressed me said that all their creeds were an abomination in his sight; that those professors were all corrupt; that: 'they draw near to me with their lips, but their hearts are far from me, they teach for doctrines the commandments of men, having a form of godliness, but they deny the power thereof.'"

modest ambition and an unworthy condescension. Joseph restored a higher way.

I marvel at the scope of Joseph's revelations. As I follow his threads, I can see truth which eludes the philosophers. The Lord showed Joseph so much more than the "Christians" know of the creation. Not only did Joseph push back the veil to the pre-mortal existence of mankind, but he took it to the very deepest levels - the initiation, the creation of the spirits of men.

Joseph defined God's glory: "The glory of God is intelligence, or, in other words, light and truth." (D&C 93: 36.) Therefore God's glory can be described as either "intelligence" or "light and truth." This glory, light and truth, or intelligence, is co-equal with God Himself. "Intelligence, or the light of truth, was not created or made, neither indeed can be." (*Id.* v. 29.) It is a part of God Himself. He and it are one. By extension, therefore, we are also one with Him.

Joseph does not leave the matter there. He goes on to equate mankind with this same material, this same co-eternal light and truth: "Man was also in the beginning with God. Intelligence, or the light of truth, was not created or made, neither indeed can be." (*Id.*) At his core, mankind is part of God. We exist because we are made of the same material from which God's glory, God's intelligence, or God's light and truth are comprised.[8]

Joseph's translation of the Book of Abraham moves from the

---

[8]It should be noted that Cleon Skousen has given another explanation of his understanding of the word "intelligences" which differs from mine. His view is accepted by many Latter-day Saints.

singular ("intelligence") to the plural in a description of pre-mortal mankind: "Now the Lord had shown unto me, Abraham, the *intelligences* that were organized before the world was; and among all these there were many of the noble and great ones; And God saw these souls that they were good, and he stood in the midst of them, and he said: These I will make my rulers; *for he stood among those that were spirits*, and he saw that they were good; and he said unto me: Abraham, thou art one of them; thou wast chosen before thou wast born." (Abr. 3: 22-23, emphasis added.)

When organized into separate personalities, the intelligence changes from the singular to the plural. With this change comes creation (or organization) and as a result, mankind came into being. Joseph further reveals that in order to exist we had to have the freedom to choose. Without that freedom we would not exist at all. We would still be singular, uncreated and without an existence. "All truth is *independent* in that sphere in which God has placed it, to *act for itself, as all intelligence also; otherwise there is no existence.*" (D&C 93: 30, emphasis added.) There is no existence unless we are free (and able) to choose for ourselves.

Our existence flows from God's intelligence. We were created from it. But to exist we must be independent from God. How, if we are part of God and emanated from Him, can we ever be "independent" from Him? This paradox is also solved by Joseph Smith. He brought the nature of eternal life, or the kind of life God has into a whole new dimension. It's true we have always had Paul's teaching: "Nevertheless neither is the man without the woman, neither the woman without the man, in the Lord." (1 Cor. 11: 11.) But this ambiguous statement has had no particular meaning for Christianity, which disavowed eternal marriage and practiced a "till death do you part" form of marital relationship for those who chose to be married. Traditional Catholic theology preferred celibacy, insisting upon it for priestly service. Joseph, on the other hand, poured meaning into this statement in a way which was unprecedented in mankind's then existing memory.

Joseph referred to a "new and everlasting covenant" involving eternal marriage and eternal increase. Speaking of heaven, Joseph wrote, "In the celestial glory there are three heavens or degrees; And in order to obtain the highest, a man must enter into this order of the priesthood [meaning the new and everlasting covenant of marriage]; And if he does not, he cannot obtain it. He may enter into the other, but that is the end of his kingdom; he cannot have an increase." (D&C 131: 1-4.) Eternal life is most correctly referred to by Joseph in revelation as "eternal lives."[9] This is because in Joseph's revelations marriage implies children and continuing creation in the afterlife. "Therefore, if a man marry him a wife in the world, and he marry her not by me nor by my word, and he

---

[9] See e.g., D&C 132: 22: "For strait is the gate, and narrow the way that leadeth unto the *exaltation and continuation of the lives*, and few there be that find it, because ye receive me not in the world neither do ye know me." (Emphasis added.) D&C 132: 24: "This is *eternal lives*--to know the only wise and true God, and Jesus Christ, whom he hath sent. I am he." (Emphasis added.) D&C 132: 55: "But ... then shall my servant Joseph do all things for her, even as he hath said; and I will bless him and multiply him and give unto him an hundredfold in this world, of fathers and mothers, brothers and sisters, houses and lands, wives and children, and crowns of *eternal lives* in the eternal worlds." (Emphasis added.)

covenant with her so long as he is in the world and she with him, their covenant and marriage are not of force when they are dead, and when they are out of the world; therefore, they are not bound by any law when they are out of the world. Therefore, when they are out of the world they neither marry nor are given in marriage; but are appointed angels in heaven, which angels are ministering servants, to minister for those who are worthy of a far more, and an exceeding, and an eternal weight of glory. For these angels did not abide my law; therefore, they cannot be enlarged, but remain separately and singly, without exaltation, in their saved condition, to all eternity; and from henceforth are not gods, but are angels of God forever and ever." (D&C 132: 15-17.) In the revelations given through Joseph Smith, creation is ongoing and meant to be shared by those who follow God's plan.

The intelligence out of which we were created might just as accurately be referred to as the "word" or the "thought" of God. In Genesis 1: 3 we read: "And God said, Let there be light: and there was light." God speaks light into existence. Or we might describe it as God imagining or conceiving light into existence. Since we are made of light, or truth, or the glory of God, it would be equally true that He conceives or imagines us into existence. It was both a creative act and an act of faith for God to conceive of us. As the Lectures on Faith put it: "[F]aith is not only the principle of action, but *of power also, in all intelligent beings, whether in heaven or on earth.* Thus says the author of the epistle to the Hebrews (11: 3): 'Through faith we understand that the worlds were framed by the word of God, so that things which are seen were not made of things which do appear.' By this we understand that *the principle of power which existed in the bosom of God, by which the worlds were framed, was faith*; and that *it is by reason of this principle of power existing in the Deity, that all created things exist; so that all things in heaven, on earth, or under the earth, exist by reason of faith as it existed in HIM.* Had it not been for the principle of faith the worlds would never have been framed, neither would man have been formed of the dust. It is the principle by which Jehovah works, and through which he exercises *power over all temporal as well as eternal things. Take this principle or attribute - for it is an attribute - from the Deity, and he would cease to exist.* Who cannot see that if God framed the worlds by faith, that it is by faith that he exercises power over them, and that faith is the principle of power? And if the principle of power, it must be so in man as well as in the Deity? This is the testimony of all the sacred writers, and the lesson which they have been endeavoring to teach to man." (*Lectures* 1: 13-17, emphasis added.) Elsewhere he added: "it is by faith that the Deity works." (*Lectures* 7: 1.)

It is absolutely essential to the process of "creation" or "conceiving" for God the Father to have a female consort or Mother God.[10] If we were the product of only one mind's thought,

---

[10]Although this conclusion is forced upon us by Joseph's revelations describing eternal life, the new and everlasting covenant of marriage, and his teachings concerning continuation of seed or offspring in the afterlife, there is no scriptural reference to a Heavenly Mother. Latter-day Saints find Her mentioned only in one official publication: the LDS Hymnal. In the Hymnal Eliza R. Snow's *O My Father*, contains this reference: "In the Heavens are parents single? No, the thought makes reason stare. Truth is reason, truth eternal, tells me I've a Mother there."

or word, or intelligence we could never act independently of the one mind. Everything about the conceived individual would be under the exclusive control of the one mind. Therefore such an individual would be wholly predictable and subordinate in all of its acts to the single mind. Only when two are jointly conceiving an individual does it become possible for the individual conceived to be independent of control. So long as both have input, neither one can fully control what the personality will choose to do. The life's choices, the story-line, the events and decisions of any given personality cannot be fully controlled by either the Father or the Mother when both are allowed to create, conceive or organize the personality. Intelligences require parents in the plural; otherwise they could not acquire independence of thought.

When the Father and Mother hold the thought (or word, or intelligence) long enough,[11] with faith in the existence of this new creation, while neither one is fully controlling the individual intelligence, then existence becomes possible. The person has everything necessary to exist in her own right. It becomes possible for the intelligence to make her own choice. Only when the intelligence accepts that right and makes a choice freely, without control by the Father and Mother, does the intelligence begin to

---

As a result, I feel no reluctance to make some limited comments on Her necessary contribution to the creation process.

[11]The limitations of language afflict this description. There is no real "time" involved in this process. However, the English language does not permit the idea to be expressed apart from the use of duration, or time to capture the thought. You must, therefore, forgive the weakness of the language used, and focus instead on the simple truth underlying it.

exist. "All truth is independent in that sphere in which God has placed it, to act for itself, as all intelligence also; otherwise there is no existence." (D&C 93: 30.) It was an act of faith by God the Father and His consort to cause the intelligence to be conceived or organized. But it requires an act of faith on the part of the intelligence to exercise her own free will to accept its creation. Unless she is free to act by making her own choice and actually does so, there is no existence.

It is difficult for created or organized intelligences to have faith in their autonomy from God, their Heavenly Parents, while they are in the presence of their Creators. They have difficulty even imagining such a thing. Christ first took this step in the pre-mortal realm. Christ showed the way for others to follow. He began the process of accepting and acting by faith, independently, proving for the rest of us the "Word" of God. We had faith in the Father's "Word" because Christ demonstrated it to be true. We acquired the faith to follow the Father because Christ's example. It does no disservice to our Heavenly Parents to attribute to Christ the whole of our existence. Heavenly Parents organized our intelligences, but it was Christ alone who proved the Word of God was faithful and true. This is why John could testify: "The worlds were made by him; *men were made by him; all things were made by him, and through him, and of him.* And I, John, bear record that I beheld his glory, as the glory of the Only Begotten of the Father, full of grace and truth, even the Spirit of truth, which came and dwelt in the flesh, and dwelt among us. And I, John, saw that *he received not of the fulness at the first, but received grace for grace; And he received not of the fulness at first, but continued from grace to grace, until he received a fulness; And thus he was called the Son of God*, because he received not of the fulness at the first." (D&C 93: 10-14, emphasis added.)

We began to accept our existence, began to act independently in the sphere in which we were placed. We were able to do this because of our faith in Christ's original example of faith. Christ led, we followed. He is correctly called our Father, even before we were born. He was the Word of God incarnate. What the Father said was possible, Christ proved by being the living example. We owe everything to our Heavenly Parents for conceiving us in the first place. But we also owe everything to the Son, who proved by faith that we could all exist. This made possible our own faith and our own independent consciousness.

Faith is an independent power beginning with God. Faith is what controls, organizes or creates all things. "It surely will not be required of us to prove that *this is the principle upon which all eternity has acted and will act*; for every reflecting mind must know that it is by reason of this power that all the hosts of heaven perform their works of wonder, majesty, and glory. Angels move from place to place by virtue of this power; it is by reason of it that they are enabled to descend from heaven to earth; and were it not for the power of faith they never could be ministering spirits to them who should be heirs of salvation, neither could they act as heavenly messengers, for they would be destitute of the power necessary to enable them to do the will of God. It is only necessary for us to say that *the whole visible creation, as it now exists, is the effect of faith. It was faith by which it was framed, and it is by the power of faith that it continues in its organized form*, and by which the planets move round their orbits and sparkle forth their glory. So, then, faith is truly the first principle in the science of THEOLOGY, and, when understood, leads the mind back to the beginning, and carries it forward to the end; or, in other words, from eternity to eternity. As *faith, then, is the principle by which the heavenly hosts perform their works*, and by which they enjoy all their felicity, we might expect to find it set forth in a revelation from God as the principle upon which his creatures here below must act in order to obtain the felicities enjoyed by the saints in the eternal world; and that, *when God would undertake to raise up men for the enjoyment of himself, he would teach them the necessity of living by faith, and the impossibility there was of their enjoying the blessedness of eternity without it, seeing that all the blessings of eternity are the effects of faith.* Therefore it is said, and appropriately too, that 'Without faith it is impossible to please God.' If it should be asked-Why is it impossible to please God without faith? The answer would be-Because without faith it is impossible for men to be saved; and *as God desires the salvation of men, he must, of course, desire that they should have faith*; and he could not be pleased unless they had, or else he could be pleased with their destruction." (*Lectures* 7: 4-7, emphasis added.)

We could not develop the kind of faith God has while living in His presence. We got as far as possible there, but to go further we needed another experience or form of existence. Since the Father wanted to move His children as organized intelligences/

personalities to a higher form of existence, a Great Plan needed to be employed. The Plan required God to create the circumstances in which it is possible for these personalities to develop the faith necessary for a higher form of existence. We learn from Joseph Smith's revelations that we are in that stage of development right now.

Joseph points us to Job for an account of our reaction when we learned the news of this Great Plan regarding our mortal experience. Job wrote of the moment when we heard we would have an opportunity to come live by faith while God remained veiled: "Where wast thou when I laid the foundations of the earth? declare, if thou hast understanding. Who hath laid the measures thereof, if thou knowest? or who hath stretched the line upon it? Whereupon are the foundations thereof fastened? or who laid the corner stone thereof; When the morning stars sang together, and all the sons of God shouted for joy?" (Job 38: 4-7.) Joseph assured us we all "shouted for joy" at the news announcing this mortal life and explaining its purpose. Joseph revealed a more complete account in Abraham 3, where we read: "Now the Lord had shown unto me, Abraham, the intelligences that were organized before the world was; and among all these there were many of the noble and great ones; And God saw these souls that they were good, and he stood in the midst of them, and he said: These I will make my rulers; for he stood among those that were spirits, and he saw that they were good; and he said unto me: Abraham, thou art one of them; thou wast chosen before thou wast born. And there stood one among them that was like unto God, and he said unto those who were with him: We will go down, for there is space there, and we will take of these materials, and we will make an earth whereon these may dwell; And we will prove them herewith, to see if they will do all things whatsoever the Lord their God shall command them; And they who keep their first estate shall be added upon; and they who keep not their first estate shall not have glory in the same kingdom with those who keep their first estate; and they who keep their second estate shall have glory added upon their heads for ever and ever." (*Id.*, vs. 22-26.) We needed this second opportunity in a new existence to develop and to be "added upon." We lacked vital understanding which could only be gained by the physical experiences here.

Mortality, or the Second Estate, is absolutely essential in the creation process, even though God continues to sustain us from moment to moment by lending us breath.[12] We all think we are independent of Him. He is so far veiled from us that everything is now reversed! It takes an act of faith to believe in His existence. We have to be taught about Him before we believe in Him. It is now more challenging to believe in *His* existence than it is to believe in our own. Mortality is the venue in which we acquire a fulsome faith in our separate existence. Even atheists are being "added upon" by

_____

[12]"God who has created you, and has kept and preserved you, and has caused that ye should rejoice, and has granted that ye should live in peace one with another--I say unto you that if ye should serve him who has created you from the beginning, and is preserving you from day to day, by lending you breath, that ye may live and move and do according to your own will, and even supporting you from one moment to another-- I say, if ye should serve him with all your whole souls yet ye would be unprofitable servants." (Mosiah 2: 20-21.)

the mortal experience; though they take their claimed independence from God too far. This second estate is brief but vital. Faith is required for daily life here.

From this second estate we all gain faith in our separate existence. Some of us will go on to develop faith sufficient to finally become self-existent beings. That is, some few will develop the faith necessary to do as all the gods have done before and to exist in our own right, under the power of our own faith, through the grace shown us by God.

Without faith it is impossible to develop properly. Proper development has the goal of making the individual personality possible to exist through his or her own faith. Until the individual has sufficient faith to exist independently, they cannot receive "all the Father has." (See D&C 84: 38.) The process of growing into self-existence requires each of us to conform to the pattern revealed by God. Since the substance from which we were originally organized was the faith, or word, or intelligence, or light and truth of God, it is impossible to become self-existent unless we conform to that light and truth, that intelligence, that faith or word of God. Self-existence flows from conforming to the purity of holiness to which all gods conform. If we are unholy, we are unworthy. We cannot contradict the light from which we originated. The great Plan of Happiness, the Gospel of Jesus Christ, the commandments, the rites, the ordinances of God (whatever terms you use to describe them) are all designed to teach us the way to conform to the perfect faith and grow in light until the perfect day. They are the path which has been taken by all of the gods. Joseph said we have to go on to learn how to become gods ourselves. Faith is essential "because without it there was no salvation, neither in this world nor in that which is to come. When men begin to live by faith they begin to draw near to God; and when faith is perfected they are like him; and because he is saved they are saved also; for they will be in the same situation he is in, because they have come to him; and when he appears they shall be like him, for they will see him as he is." (Lectures 7: 8.)

Christ is and was the Word of God because He has always conformed fully to this plan. He told us to "Come, follow Him" because He was taking those steps which would lead all of us back to the fullness. As explained by Joseph: "We ask, then, where is the prototype? or where is the saved being? We conclude, as to the answer of this question, there will be no dispute among those who believe the Bible, that it is Christ: all will agree in this, that he is the prototype or standard of salvation; or, in other words, that he is a saved being. And if we should continue our interrogation, and ask how it is that he is saved? the answer would be-because he is a just and holy being; and if he were anything different from what he is he would not be saved; for his salvation depends on his being precisely what he is and nothing else; for if it were possible for him to change, in the least degree, so sure he would fail of salvation and lose all his dominion, power, authority and glory, which constitute salvation; for salvation consists in the glory, authority, majesty, power and dominion which Jehovah possesses and in nothing else;

and no being can possess it but himself or one like him. Thus says John, in his first epistle, third chapter, second and third verses: 'Beloved, now are we the sons of God, and it doth not yet appear what we shall be; but we know that, when he shall appear, we shall be like him, for we shall see him as he is. And every man that hath this hope in him purifieth himself, even as he is pure.' Why purify themselves as he is pure? Because if they do not they cannot be like him." (Lectures 7: 9.)

While the faith to become self-existent can be demonstrated, explained, or taught: it cannot be given! It must grow within each individual. God can urge us on like a parent, but we must take the flight alone. Although this Second Estate is perfectly organized to allow us to develop faith in our own independence, it is also perfectly organized to allow us to develop the capacity to choose for ourselves whether we will use our separate existence to voluntarily follow the Plan of Happiness—the path of self-existence—the path of the Gods. If we can conceive of ourselves as separate from God, but we reject His ways, we cannot become self-existent. To be like Him we must follow His path. It would be a contradiction for us to rebel against the light from which we came and then expect we can become light itself. There are limits set which we cannot pass. When we obtain any blessing, in time or eternity, it is by conforming to the conditions associated with the blessing.[13] We must conform to the

---

[13]"Whatever principle of intelligence we attain unto in this life, it will rise with us in the resurrection. And if a person gains more knowledge and intelligence in this life through his diligence and obedience than another, he will have so much the advantage in the world to come. There is a law, irrevocably decreed in heaven before the foundations of this

truth, the pattern given to us by God in order to be true to our core. God is in our core. He is now sustaining us from moment to moment. Without Him we would not exist at all. But He intends for us to become like Him.

We come from light and truth, or intelligence. We exist as intelligences or spirits because we have the ability to act for ourselves. We are able to make our own choices. We must choose the pattern which conforms to God's revealed path or we will never develop the necessary faith to exist eternally. God is at our core, and we cannot betray that inner holiness without damage to ourselves. When we conform to the light or intelligence, we grow in exactly the attributes which give God power. "He that keepeth his commandments receiveth truth and light, until he is glorified in truth and knoweth all things." (D&C 93: 28.)

These concepts lie at the heart of many esoteric traditions. From the Kaballa to Masonry, and Neo-Platonic philosophy to Historic Christian theology. All these traditions ask: Why did God create this universe and how did He do so. Despite some answers in these other traditions' endless debate appearing superficially similar to what God revealed through Joseph, the truth belongs in the Restored Gospel of Jesus Christ. These other traditions have echoes of the truth left from earlier dispensations of the Gospel. However, none of them fully preserve the truth restored through Joseph Smith. It may be interesting to read the answers suggested by other

---

world, upon which all blessings are predicated--And when we obtain any blessing from God, it is by obedience to that law upon which it is predicated." (D&C 130: 18-21.)

philosophies or faiths, but the completed truth lies in the faith restored through Joseph. That faith, our faith, includes ALL truth. That is not to say we have completed gathering together the truths which belong to our faith. Indeed, we have some difficulty in preserving some of the truths we once received through Joseph.

There are some questions Joseph would not answer. There were things he told us he was forbidden from answering. But invariably he suggested we ask God and get answers for ourselves.[14] In this book we are going to explore more of the pattern back to God's presence revealed through Joseph Smith. The Book of Enos from the Book of Mormon has been chosen because it is a short book containing deep doctrine and important patterns. Without a lot of pages we can cover a lot of existing truth just by commenting on Enos' record. So we return again to the Book of Mormon to find just how right Joseph was. You can get closer God by abiding its precepts than any other book.

---

[14]See e.g., D&C 76: 113-118: "This is the end of the vision which we saw, which we were commanded to write while we were yet in the Spirit. But great and marvelous are the works of the Lord, and the mysteries of his kingdom which he showed unto us, which surpass all understanding in glory, and in might, and in dominion; *Which he commanded us we should not write* while we were yet in the Spirit, and are *not lawful for man to utter*; Neither is man capable to make them known, for they are only to be seen and understood by the power of the Holy Spirit, *which God bestows on those who love him*, and purify themselves before him; *To whom he grants this privilege of seeing and knowing for themselves*; That through the power and manifestation of the Spirit, while in the flesh, they may be able to bear his presence in the world of glory." (Emphasis added.)

Chapter 2

THE QUEST BEGINS

There are many different levels at which we can read our scriptures. To some extent the way we interpret any given passage is as much a reflection on the reader as it is on the writer. Therefore, it is presumptuous for anyone to ever claim he offers an exhaustive interpretation of scripture. We are limited to providing information at the level of our own limited understanding. This book studies a second generation Book of Mormon writer named Enos. He is the grandson of Lehi, nephew of Nephi, and son of Jacob. The interpretation offered here is but one way to view this early Book of Mormon writer. There are certainly others. As you consider this interpretation I am hopeful you will see at least a few things you have not considered before. To understand the Book of Mormon it is necessary for you to study the book yourself. Commentaries such as this are not adequate for the message you will find in this volume of scripture.

Before reading this book I strongly recommend you be acquainted with my earlier book *The Second Comforter: Conversing With the Lord Through the Veil.* There are many concepts explained there which we assume you understand as you read this book. *Beloved Enos* makes no attempt to reiterate those necessary foundational concepts.

"Why Enos?" is a good question. After all he is only a minor writer in the Book of Mormon. His entire content occupies but two and a half pages. However, he writes from such a fundamentally different vantage point than prior writers that it requires a different method of reading his material. No other writer in the Book of Mormon exhibits Enos' skill in composing sacred narrative.

Enos effortlessly weaves symbols into his narrative with unrivaled mastery. He is adept at employing words with caution, deliberation and skill. An entire landscape of understanding can be concealed from view in what Enos writes if the reader is not familiar with the subjects treated with symbolism. This is purposeful. By the time Enos began to write on the small plates of Nephi they were nearly full. He conserves space by reducing his words. It is easy to miss how carefully he has written when you pass over his material quickly. Slowing the pace and considering each word rewards the reader of Enos more than perhaps any other Book of Mormon author.

No doubt Enos sought to reduce fifty words to a short phrase. Then he obviously worked to reduce the short phrases to a single word, wherever possible. By the time he etched his words into the Small Plates of Nephi, he has given us an account which ought to be studied with great care to discover his intent.

The book of Enos had no editorial abridgement by Mormon. The book is part of the Small Plates which were attached in an unedited form by Mormon to his abridgment of the other writers.[15]

_____

[15]See W of M 1: 6-7: "But behold, I shall take these [small plates of Nephi], which contain these prophesyings and revelations, and put them with the remainder of my record, for they are choice unto me; and I know they will be choice unto my brethren. And I do this for a wise

As a result, the material is transmitted from Enos' hand through Joseph Smith's translation, without any alteration by anyone. Joseph Smith's translation was accomplished through the gift and power of God. We know this because Joseph declared it to be so.[16] In addition, the Three Witnesses to the Book of Mormon testified that *God* also declared it.[17] Enos' words come to us from Enos through a single, inspired translation into English. Therefore we can confidently rely upon even the most subtle of nuances found in his book.

Beloved Enos is the only book to date exclusively devoted to Enos' record. He gets mentioned in many reference works on the Book of Mormon, but he has not been singled out for a book before now. As a result, Enos has been given only passing mention rather than the tremendous respect his artful writing deserves. This book is an attempt to correct that.

This book assumes Enos held Melchizedek Priesthood, having

purpose; for thus it whispereth me, according to the workings of the Spirit of the Lord which is in me. And now, I do not know all things; but the Lord knoweth all things which are to come; wherefore, he worketh in me to do according to his will." When Mormon's original abridgement (which resulted in a hand-written translation of 116 pages) was lost, Joseph substituted the unabridged small plates of Nephi for the missing abridged pages Mormon originally included. Enos' record was among these substituted, unabridged materials.

[16]*DHC* 4: 537: "These records were engraven on plates which had the appearance of gold, each plate was six inches wide and eight inches long, and not quite so thick as common tin. They were filled with engravings, in Egyptian characters, and bound together in a volume as the leaves of a book, with three rings running through the whole. ... Through the medium of the Urim and Thummim I translated the record by the gift and power of God."

[17]The testimony of the Three Witnesses includes this declaration: "[W]e also know that they have been translated by the gift and power of God, for his voice hath declared it unto us."

received it through his lineage to Lehi. There are scholars who doubt that to be the case.[18] I accept uncritically Joseph Smith's comment: "Answer to the question, Was the Priesthood of Melchizedek taken away when Moses died? All Priesthood is Melchizedek, but there are different portions or degrees of it. That portion which brought Moses to speak with God face to face was taken away; but that which brought the ministry of angels remained. **All the prophets had the Melchizedek Priesthood and were ordained by God himself.**" (*TPJS* p. 180-181, emphasis added.) Joseph's comment suggests that Lehi, as a prophet, (See 1 Ne. 1: 18) who had been commissioned to warn Jerusalem, would be included among those who held Melchizedek authority as a necessary precondition to his calling as an Old Testament era prophet. The notion that Nephite prophets held priesthood and their authority was Melchizedek is further buttressed by the sermon of Alma on foreordination to priestly service found in Alma, Chapter 13. This book assumes Enos was a Melchizedek Priest, and was familiar with the sacred rites associated with the full functioning of that authority.

One final thought before turning to the text of Enos: Although he had an intimate relationship with the Lord, it would be wrong to view that relationship apart from Enos' character. His relationship with the Lord resulted from his charity toward others, including his enemies. Doctrine is always less important than a person's

---

[18]See e.g., John L. Sorenson's article *Religious Groups and Movements Among the Nephites, 200-1B.C.*, found on pp. 163-208 in the volume *The Disciple as Scholar: Essays on Scripture and the Ancient World in Honor of Richard Lloyd Anderson*. Edited by Steven D. Ricks, Donald W. Parry, and Andrew H. Hedges. Provo: FARMS, 2000. He writes on p. 175: "Jewish religion at the time of Lehi still allowed certain ritual practices to be carried out legitimately by nonpriests. We are not surprised, then, to read that Lehi built, in the wilderness, an altar of stones on which he sacrificed (see 1 Ne. 2: 7 and 5: 9)."

character. Although you may have a deep understanding of doctrine, if you lack charity toward others your understanding will be of no benefit.

Enos' book begins with this opening comment:

> 1 Behold, it came to pass that I, Enos, knowing my father that he was a just man--for he taught me in his language, and also in the nurture and admonition of the Lord--and blessed be the name of my God for it–

This is part of a formula first adopted by Nephi.[19] The formula calls for acknowledging parental worthiness, suitable teaching in the language of scripture, and acknowledging God's involvement in the writer's life. Enos changes the order of God's involvement, and his father's teachings. Nephi describes his life's learning as: "having seen many afflictions in the course of my days, nevertheless, having been highly favored of the Lord in all my days[.]" Enos describes his as having been raised in "the nurture and admonition of the Lord[.]" Nephi draws attention to "afflictions" first, then to having been "highly favored." In contrast, Enos draws attention first to "nurture," and second to "admonition." Nephi could see the overriding hand of Providence in the afflictions he endured. He acknowledges God's hand in all that he suffered. He was the better for having passed through his life's ordeals. God's hand in Enos' life was more gentle. He needed admonition, as we all do. However, he was perhaps a more willing student, or a more optimistic personality than Nephi. Whatever accounts for this difference, Nephi's formula

---

[19] 1 Ne. 1: 1: "I, Nephi, having been born of goodly parents, therefore I was taught somewhat in all the learning of my father; and having seen many afflictions in the course of my days, nevertheless, having been highly favored of the Lord in all my days; yea, having had a great knowledge of the goodness and the mysteries of God, therefore I make a record of my proceedings in my days."

includes "afflictions" first, and God's "favor" second, while Enos follows the formula but adopts "nurture" first, and only secondly "admonition." So, in the very beginning verse we find a contrast between Enos and the first writer in the Book of Mormon.

The fact Enos followed the formula tells us something about him. The fact he inverted the order tells us even more. He is willing to follow faithfully, but he is not going to surrender his own view of life to anyone. Enos is his own man. He has his own view. When we read him we are not reading a shrinking violet, but a man of strong convictions who will proceed with his own viewpoint.

In his next statement he transports his record into another setting altogether. He wastes no time. He employs an image with great symbolic intent:

> 2 And I will tell you of the wrestle which I had before God, before I received a remission of my sins.

He uses the interesting word "wrestle." We have but few uses of this word in all of scripture.[20] Enos ties "wrestle" to a remission of sins. As he goes on to describe the wrestle, he adds elements as follows:

> 3-5: Behold, I went to hunt beasts in the forests; and the words which I had often heard my father speak concerning eternal life, and the joy of the saints, sunk deep into my heart. And my soul hungered; and I kneeled down before my Maker, and I cried unto him in mighty prayer and supplication for mine own soul; and all the day long did I cry unto him; yea, and when the night came I

---

[20]In the King James Version of the Bible, the word "wrestle" or "wrestled" appears only in Gen. Chapters 30 and 32, of the Old Testament and in Eph. Chapter 6 of the New Testament. The one reference analogous to Enos' use appears in Chapter 32 of Genesis.

did still raise my voice high that it reached the
heavens. And there came a voice unto me, saying:
Enos, thy sins are forgiven thee, and thou shalt be
blessed.

He places his story in the forest; a place apart. He describes his
activities as "prayer and supplication" which lasts through the day
into the night. His description of the event concludes by describing
contact between himself and God. Through that contact, he
receives a remission of his sins.

There is another description of a "wrestle" between man and
God analogous to Enos'. In the other account the setting is also a
lone place apart. Jacob's encounter also lasts into the night, and
similarly includes contact between the man and God. Jacob's
wrestle is recorded in these terms:

And Jacob was left alone; and there wrestled a man
with him until the breaking of the day. And when
he saw that he prevailed not against him, he
touched the hollow of his thigh; and the hollow of
Jacob's thigh was out of joint, as he wrestled with
him. And he said, Let me go, for the day breaketh.
And he said, I will not let thee go, except thou bless
me. And he said unto him, What is thy name? And
he said, Jacob. And he said, Thy name shall be
called no more Jacob, but Israel: for as a prince hast
thou power with God and with men, and hast
prevailed. And Jacob asked him, and said, Tell me,
I pray thee, thy name. And he said, Wherefore is it
that thou dost ask after my name? And he blessed
him there. And Jacob called the name of the place
Peniel: for I have seen God face to face, and my life
is preserved. (Gen. 32: 24-30.)

We must conclude Enos intended to write these similarities into
his record. These are deliberate parallels. Beyond the parallels,

however, there are elements which anyone familiar with the fullness of the Gospel will recognize. Jacob weaves into his account the following list:

· Solitary setting
· Contact with Deity
· An embrace between God and man
· Reference to his sinews and loins
· Bestowal of a new name

The implications are clear. Jacob's narrative is deliberately including ritual symbols involved in Temple rites. Some things are sacred and cannot be spoken directly. But symbols which remind us of the sacred are entirely appropriate. Symbols are used in the Genesis account of creation to both conceal and reveal at the same moment. Christ would remind those He taught they needed to have "eyes to see" if they were to understand His teachings.[21] He taught at different levels. Those who could not grasp the depth of His stories were left unaccountable for hidden knowledge. But those who could "see" the underlying truths of His teachings were able to be informed without being forced to see. When ready, it opens to the pupil's view. When not ready, it stays veiled. In this respect Christ was a gifted and merciful teacher.

Joseph taught the ordinances of the Gospel have always been the same. The Gospel has been the same since the beginning of time. Those who lived anciently were taught the same things as we are taught, including our most sacred ordinances.[22] It should not

---

[21]See e.g., Matt. 13: 15-16; Mark 8: 18; John 12: 40.

[22]DHC 2: 16 – 17: "It is said by Paul in his letter to the Hebrew brethren, that Abel obtained witness that he was righteous, God testifying of his gifts. To whom did God testify of the gifts of Abel, was it to Paul? We have very little on this important subject in the forepart of the Bible. But it is said that Abel himself obtained witness that he was righteous.

Then certainly God spoke to him: indeed, it is said that God talked with him; and if He did, would He not, seeing that Abel was righteous, deliver to him the whole plan of the Gospel. And is not the Gospel the news of the redemption? How could Abel offer a sacrifice and look forward with faith on the Son of God for a remission of his sins and not understand the Gospel? The mere shedding of the blood of beasts or offering anything else in sacrifice, could not procure a remission of sins, except it were performed in faith of something to come; if it could, Cain's offering must have been as good as Abel's. *And if Abel was taught of the coming of the Son of God, was he not taught also of His ordinances? We all admit that the Gospel has ordinances, and if so, had it not always ordinances, and were not its ordinances always the same?* Perhaps our friends will say that the Gospel and its ordinances were not known till the days of John, the son of Zacharias, in the days of Herod, the king of Judea. But we will here look at this point: *For our own part we cannot believe that the ancients in all ages were so ignorant of the system of heaven as many suppose, since all that were ever saved, were saved through the power of this great plan of redemption, as much before the coming of Christ as since*; if not, God has had different plans in operation (if we may so express it), to bring men back to dwell with Himself; and this we cannot believe, since there has been no change in the constitution of man since he fell; and the ordinance or institution of offering blood in sacrifice, was only designed to be performed till Christ was offered up and shed His blood-as said before-that man might look forward in faith to that time. It will be noticed that, according to Paul, (see Gal. 3:8) the Gospel was preached to Abraham. We would like to be informed in what name the Gospel was then preached, whether it was in the name of Christ or some other name. If in any other name, was it the Gospel? *And if it was the Gospel, and that preached in the name of Christ, had it any ordinances? If not, was it the Gospel? And if it had ordinances what were they?* Our friends may say, perhaps, that there were never any ordinances except those of offering sacrifices before the coming of Christ, and that it could not be possible for the Gospel to have been administered while the law of sacrifices of blood was in force. But we will recollect that *Abraham offered sacrifice, and notwithstanding this, had the Gospel preached to him.* That the offering of sacrifice was only to point the mind forward to Christ, we infer from these remarkable words of Jesus to the Jews: 'Your Father Abraham rejoiced to see my day, and he saw it, and was glad' (John 8:56.) So, then, because the ancients offered sacrifice it did not hinder their hearing the Gospel; but served, as we said before, to open their eyes, and enable them to look forward to the time of the coming of the Savior, and rejoice in His redemption. We find also, that when the Israelites came out of Egypt they had the Gospel preached to them, according to Paul in his letter to the Hebrews, which says: 'For unto surprise us that Enos was able to incorporate symbols in his narrative which tie to symbols we would recognize.

Just like Jacob, Enos also demonstrates a similar capacity to employ sophisticated symbolism woven into his narrative to capture hidden meanings. He weaves into his account the following list:

·   Solitary setting in the forest, suggesting Eden
·   Contact between him and Deity
·   A conversation between God and man
·   Reference to animal sacrifice
·   A reminder of eternal life and the joy of the saints
·   Bestowal of a new name

The implications are clear enough: Enos is serving us notice that his record is intended to be read as a hermetic text.[23] He is using symbols to communicate in few words a larger meaning. He expects us to employ these symbols and their meanings as readers of his account.

So we need to consider carefully his use of images. When he writes, "I went to hunt beasts in the forests" we should keep in mind what he tells us later about the herds of domesticated animals kept among his people. He explains in verse 21 that "the people of Nephi did till the land, and raise all manner of grain, and of fruit, and flocks of herds, and flocks of all manner of cattle of every kind, and goats, and wild goats, and also many horses." He did not need

---

us was the Gospel preached, as well as unto them: but the word preached did not profit them, not being mixed with faith in them that heard it' (see Heb. 4:2). *It is said again, in Gal. 3:19, that the law (of Moses, or the Levitical law) was 'added' because of transgression. What, we ask, was this law added to, if it was not added to the Gospel? It must be plain that it was added to the Gospel, since we learn that they had the Gospel preached to them."* (Emphasis added.)

[23]Hermetic texts use symbols to conceal full meanings from the uninitiated, but which fully inform the initiated.

to "hunt" to have meat. Why mention this setting in the forest where he is engaged in hunting beasts in connection with his remembering "eternal life and the joy of the saints?"

Enos' father ministered in the Temple.[24] As a result, Enos would have Temple knowledge passed to him directly from inside his family. His introduction included reference to his father being a just man who taught him. Here Enos elaborates that "the words which I had often heard my father speak concerning eternal life, and the joy of the saints, sunk deep into my heart." Note what Enos is meditating upon has nothing to do with guilt, remorse or regret. It is purely positive; purely the highest of aspirations found in the Gospel. Enos is on a quest. He tells us what his quest involves. He is seeking after "eternal life, and the joy of the saints."

Enos' account continues with this description: "And my soul hungered; and I kneeled down before my Maker, and I cried unto him in mighty prayer and supplication for mine own soul; and all the day long did I cry unto him; yea, and when the night came I did still raise my voice high that it reached the heavens." So what did Enos' petition include? How would he have continued these many hours in this lengthy "prayer and supplication" for his own soul? Was there a ceremony involved here as a part of the "supplication" process? It becomes apparent Enos combined elements of worship to communicate something profound. He sets the events in an

---

[24]See e.g., Jacob 1: 17: "Wherefore I, Jacob, gave unto them these words *as I taught them in the temple*, having first obtained mine errand from the Lord." Jacob 2: 2: "Now, my beloved brethren, I, Jacob, according to the responsibility which I am under to God, to magnify mine office with soberness, and that I might rid my garments of your sins, *I come up into the temple this day* that I might declare unto you the word of God." Jacob 2: 11: "Wherefore, I must tell you the truth according to the plainness of the word of God. For behold, as I inquired of the Lord, thus came *the word unto me, saying: Jacob, get thou up into the temple* on the morrow, and declare the word which I shall give thee unto this people." (Emphasis added.)

Eden-like site. He tells us the object he had in mind was eternal life and the joy of the saints. He includes as part of the description performing animal sacrifice. He adds he, "raise[d] my voice high that it reached the heavens." This could not mean the decibel volume of his speaking, because from the time of Babel mankind has been on notice that heaven cannot be accessed using physical means. It must instead refer to the power of the content of the words being spoken. Everything about this suggests a most sacred and ritual meaning. Enos' words soared. They were lofty. They were sacred. They were holy. They reached into heaven itself.

Enos, the son of the Temple priest Jacob, is telling of his own endowment of power from on high. His wrestle with the Lord results in the washing away of his sin, or his anointing with the Spirit, and of his acquaintance with God.

As Enos succeeds in aligning the things of heaven with the things of earth, the veil dividing these two moves apart. In response to his petition "there came a voice unto me, saying: Enos, thy sins are forgiven thee, and thou shalt be blessed." Enos' wrestle has succeeded. He has come to the veil hiding the pavilion of God, knocked in the proper way, and been admitted.

He receives a new name. "Thou shalt be blessed" might be punctuated: "Thou shalt be: Blessed." We will discuss "blessed" as a proper noun or title later in this book.

In this contact with God, Enos refers to the "voice" which came to him. However, in another few words he will refer to what he has "heard and seen" in this encounter. Enos knows how to selectively include the right mix of symbols to inform those with the eyes to see what sacred things are unfolding in his narrative. He writes very differently from his father Jacob or his uncle Nephi. We are encountering an adept mystic; familiar with the symbols of righteousness; writing for a select audience. Five verses into his book, and we have already encountered a universe of symbols with hermetic meaning.

This is not a solitary hunting trip. Nor is this just a foray into the forest. He is writing something profound and sacred which includes symbolic allusion to Melchizedek Priestly rites and ordinances. His record is meant to be understood through "eyes which can see."

Chapter 3

THE ENDOWMENT OF POWER

In Enos' encounter with God he writes:

> 5 And there came a voice unto me, saying: Enos,
> thy sins are forgiven thee, and thou shalt be blessed.

The response contains two separate assurances. First, Enos' sins are forgiven and second, he shall be blessed. These two different statements require us to understand why Enos has etched them as he has.

The Lord cannot visit with the unclean. Alma 45: 16 teaches "for the Lord cannot look upon sin with the least degree of allowance."[25] We should not expect to find Him visiting with someone whose sins are unforgiven.

Joseph Smith gave several different accounts of the First Vision. He includes the fact that his sins were forgiven as a part of many of them. In his 1832 account he wrote: "I saw the Lord and he spake unto me saying 'Joseph, my son, thy sins are forgiven thee.'"

---

[25]We also find in D&C 1: 31: "For I the Lord cannot look upon sin with the least degree of allowance;"

(Spellings and punctuation normalized.) In his 1835 account he reported: "A personage appeared in the midst of this pillar of flame, which was spread all around and yet nothing consumed. Another personage soon appeared like unto the first; he said unto me "thy sins are forgiven thee."[26] (Punctuation normalized.)

Orson Pratt's account of Joseph's First Vision included this: "he was enwrapped in a heavenly vision, and saw two glorious personages, who exactly resembled each other in their features or likeness. He was informed that his sins were forgiven."

Although the reference concerning the remission of Joseph's sins was omitted from the account contained in the Pearl of Great Price, forgiveness was in fact a part of his first encounter with the Father and His Son. The Lord cannot "look upon sin." Therefore, He removes it by forgiving those who come into His presence. Joseph commented on the Lord's willingness to forgive in these words: "Our heavenly Father is more liberal in His views, and boundless in His mercies and blessings, than we are ready to believe or receive[.]" (*TPJS* p. 256.)

We see a consistency between the Lord's statement to Enos on the one hand and His statement to Joseph on the other. In other scriptures the Lord forgives those to whom He speaks as part of the necessary rite. For example, in a revelation given to Emma Smith, we find the Lord readily forgiving her: "Behold, thy sins are

[26]The varying accounts of the First Vision can be found in *Joseph Smith's First Vision* written by Milton V. Backman, Second Edition. Salt Lake City: Bookcraft, 1971.

forgiven thee, and thou art an elect lady, whom I have called."
(D&C 25: 3.) Similarly, when speaking to the Church in a revelation
given in late September, 1830, a few days prior to a conference, the
Lord forgives those receiving the revelation: "Behold, verily, verily,
I say unto you, that at this time your sins are forgiven you, therefore
ye receive these things; but remember to sin no more, lest perils
shall come upon you." (D&C 29: 3.) It is an almost invariable
occurrence when the Lord speaks directly to anyone that He
forgives their sins.[27] He follows the same pattern when dealing with

---

[27]See e.g., D&C 31: 5: "Therefore, thrust in your sickle with all
your soul, and your sins are forgiven you, and you shall be laden with
sheaves upon your back, for the laborer is worthy of his hire. Wherefore,
your family shall live." D&C 36: 1: "Thus saith the Lord God, the Mighty
One of Israel: Behold, I say unto you, my servant Edward, that you are
blessed, and your sins are forgiven you, and you are called to preach my
gospel as with the voice of a trump[.]" D&C 50: 36: "And behold, verily
I say unto you, blessed are you who are now hearing these words of mine
from the mouth of my servant, for your sins are forgiven you." D&C 60:
7: "And in this place let them lift up their voice and declare my word with
loud voices, without wrath or doubting, lifting up holy hands upon them.
For I am able to make you holy, and your sins are forgiven you." D&C 61:
2: "Behold, verily thus saith the Lord unto you, O ye elders of my church,
who are assembled upon this spot, whose sins are now forgiven you, for
I, the Lord, forgive sins, and am merciful unto those who confess their
sins with humble hearts[.]" D&C 62: 3: "Nevertheless, ye are blessed, for
the testimony which ye have borne is recorded in heaven for the angels
to look upon; and they rejoice over you, and your sins are forgiven you."
D&C 64: 3: "There are those among you who have sinned; but verily I
say, for this once, for mine own glory, and for the salvation of souls, I
have forgiven you your sins." D&C 90: 1: "Thus saith the Lord, verily,
verily I say unto you my son, thy sins are forgiven thee, according to thy
petition, for thy prayers and the prayers of thy brethren have come up
into my ears." D&C 90: 6: "And again, verily I say unto thy brethren,
Sidney Rigdon and Frederick G. Williams, their sins are forgiven them
also, and they are accounted as equal with thee in holding the keys of this
last kingdom[.]" D&C 95: 1: "Verily, thus saith the Lord unto you whom
I love, and whom I love I also chasten that their sins may be forgiven, for

any of us. We are unworthy. We need fixing. He repairs us so as to make it possible for us to receive an audience with Him. Enos accurately describes the manner in which the Lord deals with us all as a part of his record of the Lord's encounter with him.

This was also the pattern when the Lord healed the infirm during His mortal ministry. We read how the Lord forgave sins as He healed bodies. In the case of a palsied man brought to Him for healing, the Lord first made it clear the man's sins were forgiven him, and thereafter healed him. Matthew records the incident in these words: "And, behold, they brought to him a man sick of the palsy, lying on a bed: and Jesus seeing their faith said unto the sick of the palsy; Son, be of good cheer; thy sins be forgiven thee. And, behold, certain of the scribes said within themselves, This man blasphemeth. And Jesus knowing their thoughts said, Wherefore think ye evil in your hearts? For whether is easier, to say, Thy sins be forgiven thee; or to say, Arise, and walk? But that ye may know that the Son of man hath power on earth to forgive sins, (then saith he to the sick of the palsy,) Arise, take up thy bed, and go unto thine house. And he arose, and departed to his house. But when the multitudes saw it, they marvelled, and glorified God, which had

---

with the chastisement I prepare a way for their deliverance in all things out of temptation, and I have loved you[.]" D&C 108: 1: "Verily thus saith the Lord unto you, my servant Lyman: Your sins are forgiven you, because you have obeyed my voice in coming up hither this morning to receive counsel of him whom I have appointed." D&C 110: 5: "Behold, your sins are forgiven you; you are clean before me; therefore, lift up your heads and rejoice." D&C 112: 3: "Nevertheless, inasmuch as thou hast abased thyself thou shalt be exalted; therefore, all thy sins are forgiven thee."

given such power unto men." (Matt. 9: 2-8.)

Christ tried in vain to convince the religious leaders of His day about the relationship between inner cleanliness and spiritual power. "Woe unto you, scribes and Pharisees, hypocrites! for ye make clean the outside of the cup and of the platter, but within they are full of extortion and excess. Thou blind Pharisee, cleanse first that which is within the cup and platter, that the outside of them may be clean also." (Matt. 23: 25-26.) If these religious teachers wanted to eliminate their own spiritual failings it could never come from ceremonial observance alone. Their sins had to first be forsaken. It was Christ, of course, who was the key to accomplishing it. These blind guides were unable to see who it was speaking to them. Such is the irony frequently apparent when the religious interact with the Lord's chosen.

James tied healing to forgiveness of sins. He wrote: "Is any sick among you? let him call for the elders of the church; and let them pray over him, anointing him with oil in the name of the Lord: And the prayer of faith shall save the sick, and the Lord shall raise him up; and if he have committed sins, they shall be forgiven him." (James 5: 14-15.) Bodily healing reflects a deeper spiritual healing which invariably accompanies the presence of the Spirit. To be "visited" is to be cleaned.

Alma refers to this when performing missionary work among the Lamanites. Just prior to the slaying of the converted people of King Lamoni, they took counsel about how grateful they were at the forgiveness of their sins. Describing how the sins had been forgiven, the king said: "Oh, how merciful is our God! And now behold, since it has been as much as we could do to get our stains taken away from us, and our swords are made bright, let us hide them away that they may be kept bright, as a testimony to our God at the last day, or at the day that we shall be brought to stand before him to be judged, that we have not stained our swords in the blood of our brethren since *he imparted his word unto us and has made us clean thereby.*" (Alma 24: 15, emphasis added.) By speaking to them He made them clean. Or, more clearly, to make it possible for Him to speak with them, He forgave them because He could not tolerate any degree of sinfulness.

We can sense that as it happens. No one has ever come into the Lord's presence without a keen awareness of their sins. Isaiah described his own anxiety at meeting the Lord. The encounter, and the ceremonial remedy Isaiah obtained reads: "In the year that king Uzziah died I saw also the Lord sitting upon a throne, high and lifted up, and his train filled the temple. Above it stood the seraphims: each one had six wings; with twain he covered his face, and with twain he covered his feet, and with twain he did fly. And one cried unto another, and said, Holy, holy, holy, is the Lord of hosts: the whole earth is full of his glory. And the posts of the door moved at the voice of him that cried, and the house was filled with smoke. Then said I, Woe is me! for I am undone; because I am a man of unclean lips, and I dwell in the midst of a people of unclean lips: for mine eyes have seen the King, the Lord of hosts. Then flew one of the seraphims unto me, having a live coal in his hand, which he had taken with the tongs from off the altar: And he laid it upon my mouth, and said, Lo, this hath touched thy lips; and *thine iniquity is taken away, and thy sin purged*." (Isa. 6: 1-7, emphasis added.)

Enos' account reaffirms one of the continuing truths of Christ's Gospel. We need to be forgiven to be redeemed from the Fall. Christ intends to accomplish that because it is His great work and glory to do so.[28] When receiving any communication from Him, it is almost invariably accompanied by Him forgiving your sins first.

Next Enos tells us the Lord promises him "thou shalt be blessed." Words matter and this statement can be read in the future tense. Enos is not promised that he "is" blessed, but that in some future event or events he "shalt" be blessed. The full meaning of this statement requires us to consider why Enos was entreating the Lord at this particular time, under these circumstances, and what he was seeking. Without the earlier context this promise is unanchored in specific meaning.

Previously Enos tells us he was alone seeking the Lord because words had "sunk deep into his heart" about "eternal life and the joy of the saints." This pilgrimage was not just a whimsy. Words which sink "deep into the heart" require someone to "reflect on it again and again."[29] As a result of this reflection, Enos has told us he

---

[28]Moses 1: 39: "For behold, this is my work and my glory--to bring to pass the immortality and eternal life of man."

[29]Enos' description mirrors Joseph Smith's prelude to the First Vision. Joseph records he, too, thought deeply about the things he had been taught. He pondered over a passage of scripture promising knowledge to those who asked. "*Never did any passage of scripture come with more power to the heart of man* than this did at this time to mine. ... *I reflected*

wanted to have some personal assurance he too would have "eternal life" and experience the same "joy of the saints." He was there seeking a promise about his own eternal life - his hope of personal exaltation.

When the Lord assures Enos "thou shalt be blessed," he is being told something of eternal significance. It is clear Enos' calling and election are promised him. He will have the "eternal life" which he seeks. He too will know the "joy of the saints." He will be "blessed" in the way which is eternal.

The subject of calling and election is mentioned only briefly in all of scripture. Few people have ventured to write about the subject. What has been written has involved speculation and in some cases considerable error. Enos gives us an occasion to at least touch upon the subject. Joseph Smith brought this subject back to life and restored relevant knowledge about it. Before him, all scriptural references were too obscure to allow men to understand it. However, Joseph's comments were measured and limited. When referring to Peter's passage,[30] Joseph said: "Peter exhorts us to make

---

on it again and again, ... At length I came to the conclusion that I must either remain in darkness and confusion, or else *I must do as James directs, that is, ask of God*." (JS-H 1: 12-13, emphasis added.)

[30] 2 Peter 1: 5-10: "And beside this, giving all diligence, add to your faith virtue; and to virtue knowledge; And to knowledge temperance; and to temperance patience; and to patience godliness; And to godliness brotherly kindness; and to brotherly kindness charity. For if these things be in you, and abound, they make you that ye shall neither be barren nor unfruitful in the knowledge of our Lord Jesus Christ. But he that lacketh these things is blind, and cannot see afar off, and hath forgotten that he was purged from his old sins. Wherefore the rather, *brethren, give diligence to make your calling and election sure*: for if ye do these things, ye shall never

our calling and election sure. This is the sealing power[31] spoken of by Paul in other places." (*TPJS* p. 149.) Joseph added: "When the Lord has thoroughly proved him, and finds that the man is determined to serve Him at all hazards, then *the man will find his calling and his election made sure, then it will be his privilege to receive the other Comforter*, which the Lord hath promised the Saints, as is recorded in the testimony of St. John, in the 14th chapter, from the 12th to the 27th verses." (*TPJS* p. 150, emphasis added.)

Joseph also taught: "Now, there is some grand secret here, and keys to unlock the subject. Notwithstanding the apostle exhorts them to add to their faith, virtue, knowledge, temperance, etc., yet he exhorts them to make their calling and election sure. And though they had heard an audible voice from heaven bearing testimony that Jesus was the Son of God, yet he says we have a more sure word of prophecy, whereunto ye do well that ye take heed as unto a light shining in a dark place. Now, wherein could they have a more sure word of prophecy than to hear the voice of God saying, 'This is my beloved Son.' Now for the secret and grand key. Though they might hear the voice of God and know that Jesus was the Son of God, this would be no evidence that their election and calling was made sure, that they had part with Christ, and were joint heirs with Him. They

---

fall[.]" (Emphasis added.)

[31]It is the "sealing power" in two ways. First, by virtue of the restoration of sealing power, the Church has authority to perform an ordinance making promises unconditional. (See D&C 132: 19 where this is mentioned.) Second, as part of the process those who receive their calling and election are given the sealing authority.

then would want that more sure word of prophecy, *that they were sealed in the heavens and had the promise of eternal life in the kingdom of God.* Then, having this promise sealed unto them, it was an anchor to the soul, sure and steadfast. Though the thunders might roll and lightnings flash, and earthquakes bellow, and war gather thick around, yet *this hope and knowledge would support the soul in every hour of trial, trouble and tribulation.* Then knowledge through our Lord and Savior Jesus Christ is the grand key that unlocks the glories and mysteries of the kingdom of heaven." (*TPJS* p. 298, punctuation normalized, emphasis added.)

There are two different ways in which one's calling and election can become sure. One is through use of the sealing power restored to the Church, held in the fullness by the President of the High Priesthood, or President of the Church. Those keys are sufficient to allow for sealing people up to eternal life. In this way the Church and its ordinances are involved. This is alluded to in scripture, has been the subject of some commentary by Latter-day Saint writers, and has been mentioned but seldom in any official publications.

The other way is set out in scripture and does not directly involve the Church. The same Lord who delegated keys to men still holds those keys and does, from time to time, exercise them directly. Christ can and does make men's callings and election sure. It is this second method to which Enos alludes in his writing.

Joseph's early teachings on this subject do not suggest this is an ordinance performed by the Church. It is clear he originally expected Latter-day Saints would receive this promise of eternal life directly from the heavens. As Richard L. Bushman describes the original teaching:

> He did cite the scriptural phrases about making "your calling and election sure," and being "sealed with that holy Spirit of promise," along with John's reference to "another Comforter, that he may abide with you for ever." The Second Comforter, he explained, came to those who hungered and thirsted after righteousness and lived by every word of God. Receiving that Second Comforter made one's calling and election sure. When believers had shown themselves "determined to serve him at all hazard," then they would receive the other Comforter, "no more or less than the *Lord Jesus Christ* himself ... When any man obtains this last Comforter will have the personage of Jesus Christ to attend him or appear unto him from time to time." Joseph's long quest to prepare his people to see the face of God appears here again in the form of Christ dwelling with the believer. "He will manifest the Father unto him & they will take up their abode with him, & the visions of the heavens will be opened unto him & the Lord will teach him face to face & he may have a perfect knowledge of the mysteries of the kingdom of God."
>
> That emphasis on intelligence – a perfect knowledge of the mysteries coupled with the promise that hungry souls would see Christ – was classic Joseph Smith. "The day must come when no man need say to his neighbor know ye the Lord for all shall know him ... from the least to the greatest." (Bushman, Richard Lyman, *Joseph Smith: Rough Stone Rolling*. New York: Alfred A. Knopf, 2005. pp. 387-8.)

Brother Bushman takes notice of a later alteration by Joseph in the plan. According to his analysis the modification consisted of this:

> In early revelations, the word "endowment"
> referred to seeing God, a bequest of Pentecostal
> spiritual light. The use of the word "endowment" in
> Nauvoo implied that the goal of coming into God's
> presence would be realized now through ritual
> rather than transcendent vision. This transition gave
> Mormonism's search for direct access to God an
> enduring form. David Hume, the eighteenth-
> century empiricist and critic of "enthusiastic"
> religion, had observed that outbursts of visions and
> revelations soon sputtered out. They lacked form to
> keep them alive. They could not endure because
> they had "no rites, no ceremonies, no holy
> observances, which may enter into the common
> train of life, and preserve the sacred principles from
> oblivion." To remain in force, "enthusiasm" had to
> be embodied in holy practice. Ann Taves, a modern
> scholar of religion, has added that "direct
> inspiration survives only when it is supported by
> sacred mythos embedded in sacred practices." The
> Mormon temple's sacred story stabilized and
> perpetuated the original enthusiastic endowment.
> (*Id.*, p. 451.)

In this analysis Brother Bushman goes too far. Joseph never
abandoned the idea of God's authority to visit with man, nor ever
taught the Temple rites were a complete replacement of the
possibility for faithful followers receiving an audience with God.
Nor did Joseph claim the Church's rites involving the calling and
election of a person precluded such promises from coming directly
from the Lord. It would be more correct to say the Temple rites
were added to the restored faith precisely because they were
intended to teach the process by ritual, so as to *enable* the real event

involving God to occur. The Temple is not the stopping place. It is a revelation of the process by which one may pass through the veil to God's actual presence. We will revisit this later in Enos' writing.

On May 21, 1843, Joseph taught: "1st key: Knowledge is the power of salvation. 2nd key: Make your calling and election sure. 3rd key: It is one thing to be on the mount and hear the excellent voice, etc., and another to hear the voice declare to you, You have a part and lot in that kingdom." (*TPJS*, p. 306.) Enos heard that voice. Enos was told his sins were forgiven and the eternal life which he sought was his. He shall be blessed with eternal life and to share in the coveted joy of the saints. He did not need to rely upon the words of a book, or the sacred experiences recorded by others. He no longer needed to rely on the words taught by his father; those that he let sink deep into his heart. He was allowed to join into the sacred narrative himself, recording once again the voice of God speaking directly to man, promising him eternal life.

Chapter 4

THE WITNESS OF CHRIST

*E*nos' next statement is remarkable. He records:

> 6 And I, Enos, knew that God could not lie;
> wherefore, my guilt was swept away.

Again we require context for this statement to acquire its full meaning.

First, let's examine the proposition that God "could not lie." At a glance, the proposition seems beyond dispute, however it can be misleading. For example, is it a "lie" to not tell someone everything? God has done that from the beginning of this world. Can someone use words of art, that is, words having a highly specific meaning, without disclosing the specific meaning, and yet not "lie?" God has done that, as well. What does it really mean then that "God cannot lie?"

In the case of Abraham, we have this interesting account: "And it came to pass when I was come near to enter into Egypt, the Lord said unto me: Behold, Sarai, thy wife, is a very fair woman to look upon; Therefore it shall come to pass, when the Egyptians shall see her, they will say--She is his wife; and they will kill you, but they will save her alive; therefore see that ye do on this wise: Let her say unto the Egyptians, she is thy sister, and thy soul shall live. And it came to pass that I, Abraham, told Sarai, my wife, all that the Lord had said unto me--Therefore say unto them, I pray thee, thou art my sister, that it may be well with me for thy sake, and my soul shall live because of thee." (Abr. 2: 22-25.) There are many commentaries attempting to sort out the familial relationship between Abraham and Sarai.[32] It is not important to do so for our purposes. The issue is not whether we can justify the "sisterhood" of Sarai to Abraham. Rather, the issue is whether the Egyptians would be misled to believe Sarai was NOT Abraham's wife. The statement was intended to conceal the fact that Abraham was married to Sarai.

The idea of misleading the Egyptians was the Lord's. He was protecting the life of Abraham, and used a half-truth (Sarai was Abraham's sister) to conceal a greater, more relevant truth (Sarai was Abraham's wife). If incomplete, evasive answers designed to conceal something important from notice fall within the scope of the statement: "God cannot lie," then we have to be very careful about how we understand the statement. How can we ever have any confidence in the words God speaks to us if He can be so artful in parsing language? How can we know we are not being misled by part truths which conceal greater, more relevant truths?

There is another way the Lord uses the words "endless" and "eternal." These terms are used in scripture to describe damnation. The normal use of the word suggests to the mind a kind of

---

[32]Even though some attempt to explain how Sarai was Abraham's "sister" she was not so in the typical use of the term. She was the daughter of his brother Haran. When Haran died, Abraham's father raised his grandchildren (Haran's children) as his own. Two of these granddaughters married their uncles. One married Nahor (Abraham's brother), the other (Sarai) married Abraham. She was his niece and step-sister.

punishment which would never come to an end. But, the Lord explains His artful language: "And surely every man must repent or suffer, for I, God, am endless. Wherefore, I revoke not the judgments which I shall pass, but woes shall go forth, weeping, wailing and gnashing of teeth, yea, to those who are found on my left hand. Nevertheless, it is not written that there shall be no end to this torment, but it is written endless torment. Again, it is written eternal damnation; wherefore it is more express than other scriptures, that it might work upon the hearts of the children of men, altogether for my name's glory. Wherefore, I will explain unto you this mystery, for it is meet unto you to know even as mine apostles. I speak unto you that are chosen in this thing, even as one, that you may enter into my rest. For, behold, the mystery of godliness, how great is it! For, behold, I am endless, and the punishment which is given from my hand is endless punishment, for Endless is my name. Wherefore-- Eternal punishment is God's punishment. Endless punishment is God's punishment." (D&C 19: 4-12.)

The Lord is explaining this language is intended to "work upon the hearts of the children of men" so they will mistakenly fear a punishment without end. But, clearly it is not written that there would be no end to this punishment. Even though it is strongly implied, the scriptures do not say that. So once again, if God "cannot lie" but can use words to tactically mislead for a desired effect, what are we to conclude?

Christ's mortal ministry was punctuated by teachings that deliberately withheld information from those who were not initiated into understanding the mysteries He taught. He did not speak "plainly" to the disbelievers. The Gospel writers had no problem recording this tendency to reveal and conceal in His teachings. We read in Matthew the following description:

> And he spake many things unto them in parables,
> saying, Behold, a sower went forth to sow; And
> when he sowed, some seeds fell by the way side,
> and the fowls came and devoured them up: Some
> fell upon stony places, where they had not much
> earth: and forthwith they sprung up, because they
> had no deepness of earth: And when the sun was
> up, they were scorched; and because they had no
> root, they withered away. And some fell among
> thorns; and the thorns sprung up, and choked them:
> But other fell into good ground, and brought forth
> fruit, some an hundredfold, some sixtyfold, some
> thirtyfold. Who hath ears to hear, let him hear. And
> the disciples came, and said unto him, *Why speakest
> thou unto them in parables? He answered and said unto
> them, Because it is given unto you to know the mysteries of
> the kingdom of heaven, but to them it is not given.* For
> whosoever hath, to him shall be given, and he shall
> have more abundance: but whosoever hath not,
> from him shall be taken away even that he hath.
> *Therefore speak I to them in parables: because they seeing see
> not; and hearing they hear not, neither do they understand.*
> (Matt. 13: 3-13, emphasis added.)

The whole purpose of His teaching method was to mislead,
conceal, and prevent some unprepared listeners from
understanding. When He spoke candidly about His destiny to His
disciples, "His disciples said unto him, Lo, now speakest thou
plainly, and speakest no proverb." (John 16: 29.) They recognized
the difference between the Lord speaking "plainly" and speaking in
"proverbs" or parables. Again there is a certain amount of
cleverness, misdirection and deliberate confusion shown by this
kind of communication. So we need to be very clear on the meaning
used by Enos in his declaration of God's inability to "lie."

Enos is, in fact, writing about an altogether different kind of communication in which God cannot and does not lie or anything like it. He is writing about covenant-making. As to covenants, God intends to be bound, is always interested in clarity, and will construe all terms in favorably for man's benefit. He makes it clear: "What I the Lord have spoken, I have spoken, and I excuse not myself; and though the heavens and the earth pass away, my word shall not pass away, but shall all be fulfilled, whether by mine own voice or by the voice of my servants, it is the same." (D&C 1: 38.) Covenants "shall all be fulfilled" by the Lord. Even covenants made long ago, among people long since dead, whose meaning has become lost or obscure. The Lord will never offer an excuse, nor deviate in the smallest degree from what He covenants to do.

Nephi not only met the Lord, but was shown in vision all the history of the earth. As he reflected on his visionary encounter with God, what stood out among the lessons learned was how committed God is to fulfilling His covenants with mankind. Nephi wrote: "Wherefore, our father hath not spoken of our seed alone, but also of all the house of Israel, *pointing to the covenant which should be fulfilled in the latter days; which covenant the Lord made to our father Abraham*, saying: In thy seed shall all the kindreds of the earth be blessed." (1 Ne. 15: 18, emphasis added.) God's dealing with mankind through all generations has been governed by the covenants He has made. He is determined to fulfill every whit of His covenantal obligations.

Christ explained to the Nephites that even though He fulfilled the law of Moses, He had no intention of abandoning one iota of His covenants: "Behold, I am he that gave the law, and *I am he who covenanted with my people Israel*; therefore, the law in me is fulfilled, for I have come to fulfil the law; therefore it hath an end. Behold, *I do not destroy the prophets, for as many as have not been fulfilled in me, verily I say unto you, shall all be fulfilled.* And because I said unto you that old things have passed away, I do not destroy that which hath been spoken concerning things which are to come. For behold, *the covenant which I have made with my people is not all fulfilled*; but the law which was given unto Moses hath an end in me." (3 Ne. 15: 5-7.)

Christ explained how covenants govern the entire unfolding history of mankind, including the details of the end of times: "And behold, *this people will I establish in this land, unto the fulfilling of the covenant which I made with your father Jacob*; and it shall be a New Jerusalem. And the powers of heaven shall be in the midst of this people; yea, even I will be in the midst of you." (3 Ne. 20: 22, emphasis added.)

So when Enos says God "cannot lie," he is announcing certitude for the Lord's pronouncement that his sins are forgiven and he shall be eternally blessed. He knows he will have eternal life and experience the joy of the saints. This is certain. God never equivocates in any degree whatsoever about such matters. What He has spoken as a covenant will invariably come to pass throughout all generations, from time into eternity. This is why one's calling and election becomes "sure" when promised eternal life.

Next Enos writes:

7 And I said: Lord, how is it done?

This is an inspired inquiry. This is exactly what we want to know. We would all like to have eternal life. So when Enos is provoked to ask, we are able to come to a higher understanding of how these things work. The inspired inquiry is part of a pattern described in the Doctrine & Covenants: "But no man is possessor of all things except he be purified and cleansed from all sin. And *if ye are purified and cleansed from all sin, ye shall ask whatsoever you will in the name of Jesus and it shall be done.* But know this, *it shall be given you what you shall ask;*"

(D&C 50: 28-30, emphasis added). You can ask for and receive anything, when the Lord makes you the offer Enos received. However, you should be inspired or instructed what to ask. Enos' inquiry is inspired and focused upon the very issue which we need to have answered for our own eternal welfare.

The answer to this inquiry also opens a flood of wonderful new light:

> 8 And he said unto me: Because of thy faith in Christ, whom thou hast never before heard nor seen. And many years pass away before he shall manifest himself in the flesh; wherefore, go to, thy faith hath made thee whole.

There are so many truths found here we need to look at them all.

"Because of thy faith in Christ" is the first, necessary principle. Faith as used here is not mere belief. It is faith in the sense of a principle of action discussed in the Sixth Lecture on Faith.[33] The power to rend the veil comes through faith. Nephi quotes Christ in 2 Ne. 27: 23 saying: "For behold, I am God; and I am a God of miracles; and I will show unto the world that I am the same yesterday, today, and forever; and *I work not among the children of men save it be according to their faith.*" (Emphasis added.) Faith and miracles are linked. "[I]t is by faith that miracles are wrought; and it is by faith that angels appear and minister unto men; wherefore, *if these things have ceased wo be unto the children of men, for it is because of unbelief, and all is vain.* For no man can be saved, according to the words of Christ, save they shall have faith in his name; wherefore, *if these things have ceased, then has faith ceased also*; and awful is the state of man, for they are as though there had been no redemption made." (Moro. 7:

---

[33] I previously wrote about that in my prior book *The Second Comforter: Conversing With the Lord Through the Veil* (Salt Lake: Mill Creek Press; 2nd Edition 2008). For that discussion see pp. 182-199.

37-38, emphasis added.) If these sacred things have ceased, then ceremonial enactments of sacred events cannot be an adequate substitute. Ceremony testifies of the real thing but it is not the real thing. As a result we should realize the Temple is a tool and not the end in itself. Angels must minister and miracles must come or else no one is being saved. Faith which saves is never dormant. We cannot just "confess with the lips" anything more than what all, even the unbelieving, will do.[34] Enos has faith comparable to that of Abraham, as is apparent later. Such faith comes from following Christ; not only to say but to do.

We know Enos is saved. We know he does experience the miraculous and has an audience with the Lord. He got an answer to his petition. He has the promise of eternal life. And he assures us these things result from faith in Christ.

A necessary part of this faith must be centered in Christ. All miracles draw upon the power in Christ. When gifted or spiritually sensitive people ignore the connection between Christ and their gifts, they lack the faith that redeems. They may enjoy some manifestations of spiritual power as a native endowment, but unless they connect that to Christ they cannot be saved. All gifts come

---

[34]Paul wrote in Rom. 10: 9: "That if thou shalt confess with thy mouth the Lord Jesus, and shalt believe in thine heart that God hath raised him from the dead, thou shalt be saved." Then continued writing and added at Rom. 14: 11: "For it is written, As I live, saith the Lord, every knee shall bow to me, and every tongue shall confess to God." Paul's first statement has been interpreted by some to mean mere belief is sufficient for salvation. When his second comment from the same letter is added, however, it becomes clear Paul was not teaching a slovenly Gospel devoid of active faith. Given Paul's ministry, service, visions, healings, signs and evidence of daily sacrifice for his faith, it is clear he did not practice a faith comprised of confession and devoid of active, continual and tremendous works born of his faith. Fortunately, the Book of Mormon is clearer on this point, and excludes the misinterpretations imposed upon Paul.

from Him. It is He who has "created you from the beginning, and is preserving you from day to day, by lending you breath, that ye may live and move and do according to your own will, and even supporting you from one moment to another." (Mosiah 2: 21.) Whenever someone ignores Christ's role in creating and sustaining their life, they miss salvation itself. Miracles alone do not redeem or convert. Signs are not an adequate basis for salvation. Without faith centered in Christ, there is no redemption.

Enos goes on to explain his faith in Christ is in a being "whom thou hast never *before* heard nor seen." Before this moment Enos had not yet *heard* Christ. He had not previously *seen* Christ. Implicit in this statement is that Enos was now hearing and seeing Christ. His faith in Christ preceded this audience. But he now has replaced faith with knowledge of his Redeemer and Savior. He now hears His voice and knows Him. Enos is now one of the Lord's witnesses. He can testify of Him because of his knowledge of Him.

Enos will refer to *seeing* Christ twice in his record. This reference to faith in Christ, whom he had not previously seen, is followed later by a reference to "testifying of the things which I had heard and *seen*." (Verse 18, emphasis added.) Enos is discrete, but plain. If we are willing to see what he includes in his record, we see the encounters of Enos with God include seeing and hearing His Son.

Verse 8 continues:

> 8 And many years pass away before he shall manifest himself in the flesh[.]

Christ may manifest Himself to men from time to time as the scriptures tell us; but, to Enos His earthly ministry in the flesh is yet some years away. "Flesh" used in this context refers to mortality. Although Christ was a living, distinct personage at the time of Enos' encounter with Him, He would not enter the mortal arena, showing

Himself "in the flesh" for yet "many years."

We find it plausible to believe in a God who came to the earth, lived, taught, died and was resurrected. Enos, however, believed in a God who would at a future day come to the earth, live, teach, die and be resurrected. To him Christ was future. Further, Christ would come to the land from which Enos' ancestors fled. Perhaps we ought to give Enos more credit for his faith in the future ministry of the Lord than we do to ourselves for believing in an historic Savior. However, faith is the same difficult struggle for anyone living at any time. We do not have it easier; how many of us have the testimony of an Enos? He did not have it harder; for he struggled to move from belief, to faith, to knowledge in the same upward climb required of any of us. We find once again the Gospel to be the same yesterday, today and tomorrow. We see how the Lord can say: "For if ye are not equal in earthly things ye cannot be equal in obtaining heavenly things[.]" (D&C 78: 6.) We are subject to the same measure, all weighed in the same balance. None of the ancients had the advantage; none of us the disadvantage. What are you doing with your earthly probation? Would you like to pass the same test given to all mortals? That is entirely up to you. It is little wonder the Lord's parables about workers in His vineyard were rewarded "equally" for their earthly labors. "Saying, These last have wrought but one hour, and thou hast made them equal unto us, which have borne the burden and heat of the day." (Matt. 20: 12.) Christ must have loved teaching this parable. From an eternal perspective we all bear the same burden, face the same trials, and are measured against the same standard. We are encouraged to add to our faith until we obtain the perfect day, have our calling and election made sure, and like the ancients find ourselves companions of Holy Beings. The only permission needed is within the reach of even the least of us. We do not need to be called by Jerusalem (or Salt Lake), because the invitation comes from heaven itself and is extended to every one of us.

The verse concludes with the remarkable comment from the Lord to Enos: "wherefore, go to, thy faith hath made thee whole." What a fascinating comment! The idea captured in by the word "whole" is akin to the idea of being completed. Enos is no longer a work in process. He has run a good race, finished the course, and can enter into the rest of the Lord. He need have no further apprehension about his own eternal state. Anxiety over death and the eternities to follow are removed. Enos is whole. What a wonderful gift Enos has left us in this testimony!

What then, does someone who is "whole" concern himself with? Even though whole and at rest, are there other anxieties to occupy you? The answer to that question begins in the next Chapter.

Chapter 5

THE LOVE OF CHRIST

ephi was an elderly man when he etched his record onto metal plates. It is likely he recorded events as they occurred. However, etching them onto his plates was a later event. He tells us he reflected on his experiences often. (See 2 Ne. 4: 16: "Behold, my soul delighteth in the things of the Lord; and my heart pondereth continually upon the things which I have seen and heard.") The plates were the product of long reflection and mature understanding. Therefore Nephi gives us the wisdom of many years of refinement in his account.

Jacob did the same thing. He etched his account as a mature man. There is some reason to believe that Jacob did not finish his book, but that it included excerpts taken from his writing and added by Enos as a conclusion to the final verses of the Book of Jacob. However, that is beyond the scope of this work. For our purposes, it is only necessary to note that throughout the Book of Mormon the actual events and when they occurred may be widely separated from when they were etched on the plates. Therefore, when we read the accounts we ought to consider the distinct possibility that the record has time passages that are not stated outright, but merely implied. These next verses suggest the compression of time into the cryptic language employed to describe events.

Enos writes:

> 9 Now, it came to pass that when I had heard these
> words I began to feel a desire for the welfare of my
> brethren, the Nephites[.]

He "began" to feel this desire as a natural consequence of his own
"wholeness." In the Lord's presence we cannot avoid drinking in
the charity or pure love which emanates from Him. Christ's most
spiritually sensitive apostle described the Lord as love itself.[35] The
fact Enos "began to feel a desire for the welfare" of others confirms
to us the reality of his association with Christ. Joseph Smith
commented on how charity for others is the consequence of
knowing God. He put it in these words: "The nearer we get to our
heavenly Father, the more we are disposed to look with compassion
on perishing souls; we feel that we want to take them upon our
shoulders, and cast their sins behind our backs." (*TPJS* p. 241.)
Once someone knows they are an heir of salvation, they yearn to
see others join them. How can they remain quiet when their family
is unredeemed? What of their friends, neighbors, and associates?
When Enos turns his attention outward, those he notices first are
his brethren, closest in proximity to his own heart. Like concentric
circles, with Christ and Enos in the first, now the love spreads out
to the next circle of Enos' friends. Eventually the circle will widen
to even include Enos' enemies. But first, we learn of his friends:
"wherefore, I did pour out my whole soul unto God for them."

The description does not require us to read this as a single
outpouring. It is possible Enos did this over a series of days or
months. As to pouring out his whole soul, no matter the time frame

---

[35] 1 Jn. 4: 8: "He that loveth not knoweth not God; for God is
love."

involved, Enos yearned for his brethren's welfare and made intercession for them.

While in mortality Christ was asked: "which is the great commandment in the law?" He answered it was love of God and others: "Jesus said unto him, Thou shalt love the Lord thy God with all thy heart, and with all thy soul, and with all thy mind. This is the first and great commandment. And the second is like unto it, Thou shalt love thy neighbour as thyself. On these two commandments hang all the law and the prophets." (Matt. 22: 36-40.) By pouring out his heart for others, Enos showed he had captured all the law and prophets in his heart.

At the point when Enos' heartfelt struggles are completed, and his compassion for his brethren is also "whole," his intercessory efforts were acknowledged by the Lord speaking to him:

> 10 And while I was thus struggling in the spirit, behold, the voice of the Lord came into my mind again, saying[.]

This is a remarkable comment which clarifies what Enos has experienced. We should consider what Enos has just informed us.

Enos has given to us an insight into how one form of revelation occurs. Although this is playing out directly to Enos, he knows it is a voice "into [his] mind." Someone standing beside him would not know and could not hear the dialogue taking place. Joseph Smith explained how this happens in these words: "All things whatsoever God in his infinite wisdom has seen fit and proper to reveal to us, while we are dwelling in mortality, in regard to our mortal bodies, *are revealed to us in the abstract, and independent of affinity of this mortal tabernacle, but are revealed to our spirits precisely as though we had no bodies at all*; and those revelations which will save our spirits will save our bodies." (*TPJS* p. 355, emphasis added.) In the Vision of the Three Degrees of Glory (D&C 76), only Joseph Smith and Sidney Rigdon saw the vision, even though there were others in the room. The scribe who wrote down the account as it was dictated heard only Joseph's and Sidney's voices. He and the others saw only Joseph and Sidney, but nothing of the Celestial, Terrestrial, Telestial or outer darkness conditions. This is because it was not opened to the minds of these others.

Joseph's First Vision contains a similar description of how this works. When the encounter began it "entirely overcame me," wrote Joseph. (JS-H 1: 15.) When it ended, he reawakened. "When I came to myself again, I found myself lying on my back, looking up into heaven." (*Id.*, v. 20.) Someone else standing in the Sacred Grove on that particular Spring morning would have seen nothing. They could not take part in God's communication with Joseph. He was the lone recipient.

This is not to say such experiences are not experienced physically. As Paul put it: "I knew a man in Christ above fourteen years ago, (*whether in the body, I cannot tell; or whether out of the body, I cannot tell*: God knoweth;) such an one caught up to the third heaven. And I knew such a man, (*whether in the body, or out of the body, I cannot tell*: God knoweth;) How that he was caught up into paradise, and heard unspeakable words, which it is not lawful for a man to utter." (2 Cor. 12: 2-4, emphasis added.) Paul saw the Celestial abode of God; or the third heaven as he describes it. He no doubt felt tangible surface beneath his feet, saw tangible things unfolding before him, smelled the incense of heavenly courts, heard the ceremonial greetings which occur there, with such concrete and specific substance that they *were* tangible to him. This was not Paul's imagination. It was done to him. It was so physical an event he could not tell if he was taken bodily to the third heaven or only taken in the spirit.

Joseph and Oliver saw Christ in the Kirtland Temple. They describe the event in physical terms: "We saw the Lord standing upon the breastwork of the pulpit, before us; and under his feet was a paved work of pure gold, in color like amber. His eyes were as a flame of fire; the hair of his head was white like the pure snow; his countenance shone above the brightness of the sun; and his voice was as the sound of the rushing of great waters, even the voice of Jehovah, saying: I am the first and the last; I am he who liveth, I am he who was slain; I am your advocate with the Father. Behold, your sins are forgiven you; you are clean before me; therefore, lift up your heads and rejoice." (D&C 110: 2-5.) Although the description contains purely physical things (Lord standing, paved work of pure gold, eyes like fire, white hair, shining countenance), Joseph and Oliver put the entire event into context by the first verse: "The veil was taken from our minds, and the eyes of our understanding were opened." Their "minds" were opened. The "eyes of understanding" were able to see. To those who experience these things, they *are* physical while they occur. So far as either of them could tell, Christ was standing on a pure gold pavement atop a pulpit of the Kirtland Temple.

Joseph F. Smith's vision of Christ's visit to the Spirit World contains a similar statement of how the event was shown him. He wrote: "As I pondered over these things which are written, *the eyes of my understanding were opened*, and the Spirit of the Lord rested upon me, and *I saw* the hosts of the dead, both small and great." (D&C 138: 11.) He sees a shift of scenes and later adds: "And as I wondered, *my eyes were opened, and my understanding quickened*, and I perceived that the Lord went not in person among the wicked and the disobedient who had rejected the truth, to teach them[.]" (*Id.*, v. 29, emphasis added.)

Enos has used the same description to present to us the same kind of event. He hears the words of God entering into his mind.[36] He understood them with clarity even greater than words spoken by

---

[36]Elder Orson Pratt ventured into this subject in a talk given on October 22, 1859 in the Tabernacle. He taught: "For instance; how do you suppose that spirits after they leave these bodies, communicate one with another? *Do they communicate their ideas by the actual vibrations of the atmosphere the same as we do? I think not. I think if we could be made acquainted with the kind of language by which spirits converse with spirits, we would find that they do not communicate their ideas in this manner; they have a more refined way*; I mean that portion of them that are in the school of progress; they have undoubtedly a more refined system among them of communicating their ideas. This system will be so constructed that they can, not only communicate at the same moment upon one subject, as we have to do by making sounds in the atmosphere, *but communicate vast numbers of ideas, all at the same time, on a great variety of subjects; and the mind will be capable of perceiving them.* ... Well inquires one, "Can you imagine up any such system, or language in this world?" I can imagine up one, but it cannot be made practicable here, from the fact that the mind of man is unable to use it. For instance, the Book of Mormon tells us, that the angels speak by the power of the Holy Ghost, and man when under the influence of it, speaks the language of angels. Why does he speak in this language? Because the Holy Ghost suggests the ideas which he speaks; and it gives him utterance to convey them to the people. Suppose the Holy Ghost should suggest to the mind of an individual a vast multitude of truths, I mean when in the spiritual state, and he wished to convey that intelligence and knowledge to his fellow spirit; suppose, instead of having arbitrary sounds, such as we have here, to communicate these ideas, that the Holy Ghost itself, through a certain process and power, should enable him to unfold that knowledge to another spirit, all in an instant, without this long tedious process of artificial and arbitrary sounds, and written words. The fact is, if celestial spirits were so organized, and so constructed, as to close up their own ideas in their own bosoms, from those in a lower condition, or to disclose them at their own pleasure, according to the mind and wisdom of the Holy Ghost, and others were so organized and constituted as to receive these ideas by the power of the Holy Ghost, it would be just as good a communication between man and man-between spirit and spirit, as any other medium, and perhaps far better." (*JD* 3: 101 – 102.)

an audible voice.

Christ can and does appear physically, as well as in visions; when he cooked and ate beside the sea after His resurrection;[37] when he appeared in the Garden outside the tomb;[38] as He walked to Emmaus,[39] He showed Himself every bit as tangible as any of us. So we need to be careful about dogmatically claiming the capacities of resurrected beings to appear are limited to any single form. If He appears physically, He assumes one of two forms: He appears as any other mortal, like on the Road to Emmaus; or He appears as a glorified being. However, as a glorified being, He can only show Himself to men who are transfigured so as to survive His glory.

Speaking to Enos, the Lord answers his heartfelt concern for his brethren with this promise: "I will visit thy brethren according to their diligence in keeping my commandments. I have given unto them this land, and it is a holy land; and I curse it not save it be for the cause of iniquity; wherefore, I will visit thy brethren according as I have said; and their transgressions will I bring down with sorrow upon their own heads." This is the state of the Americas. It is a promised land, but will only provide security for those who follow Christ.[40] Enos' answer from the Lord mirrored what Nephi

---

[37]John 21: 9-14.

[38]John 20: 14-18.

[39]Luke 24: 13-35. Note that despite His corporeal appearance, He was also able to "vanish out of their sight." (See v. 31.)

[40]See e.g., Alma 37: 28: "For behold, there is a curse upon all this land, that destruction shall come upon all those workers of darkness, according to the power of God, when they are fully ripe; therefore I desire that this people might not be destroyed." Hel. 13: 17: "And behold, a curse shall come upon the land, saith the Lord of Hosts, because of the peoples' sake who are upon the land, yea, because of their wickedness and their abominations."

had seen earlier in vision.[41] The Nephites were (as Neal Maxwell might put it), probationary possessors of the promised land. Should they violate the conditions of their probation, they would lose the right to possess it. As a result, this answer given to Enos is only a reaffirmation of prior warnings.

Enos next writes:

> 11 And after I, Enos, had heard these words, my faith began to be unshaken in the Lord; and I prayed unto him with many long strugglings for my brethren, the Lamanites.

This raises the question of what Enos meant by unshakable faith, and why it appears in his record at this point. The answer to that is contained in Joseph Smith's testimony. Joseph had an encounter with God on a spring morning in 1820. Some years later Joseph was interested in knowing his standing before God. He petitioned the Lord, and "for a manifestation to me, that I might know of my state and standing before him; for *I had full confidence in obtaining a divine manifestation, as I previously had one.*" (JS-H 1: 29, emphasis added.) That is, Joseph would have been more surprised by *not* getting an answer than by getting one. His faith was "full confidence" or, in other words, unshakable.

Enos also had "unshakable" faith because he had already heard from the Lord. The Lord reiterated the pessimistic news about his people, which Nephi had previously recorded on the Small Plates. The Nephites had no guarantee for their future survival. Everything

---

[41]1 Ne. 12: 19-20: "And while the angel spake these words, I beheld and saw that the seed of my brethren did contend against my seed, according to the word of the angel; and *because of the pride of my seed, and the temptations of the devil, I beheld that the seed of my brethren did overpower the people of my seed.* And it came to pass that I beheld, and saw the people of the seed of my brethren that they had overcome my seed; and they went forth in multitudes upon the face of the land." (Emphasis added.)

was conditioned upon their worthiness. So long as they were obedient they would be preserved. As soon as they were not, they would be swept away. As a result, Enos had unshakable faith in two senses. First, he was fully expecting an answer from prior experience and knew the Lord would answer. Second, he had the humility to accept with faith any answer, no matter its content.

Enos tells the next part of his experience with language strongly suggesting it involved more than a single day's retreat to the forest. He writes of "many long strugglings." "Many" requires more than one, perhaps dozens, even hundreds. We cannot know if this was the work of months or years. We cannot be certain if more than a decade passed as he engaged in these "many" struggles. Whatever the time frame involved, they were not only "many" but they were also "long."

There is more going on here than just a single, brief petition to the Lord. Enos is undergoing gradual, internal changes which are significantly difficult. Enos is "struggling" because of an internal conflict over the subject of his prayers. He is confronting the Lamanite issue. His father wrote[42] at the end of his record the

---

[42]This is among the final few verses in the Book of Jacob. It is not unlikely, however, that this verse and those which followed were physically etched into the plates by Enos. The words were Jacob's but the hand which etched them were likely Enos'. Jacob had brought his record to a close, following carefully Nephi's entire formula for record writing, at the end of Chapter 6. He even bids the readers farewell until he "shall meet you before the pleasing bar of God" (Jacob 6: 13) just as Nephi did (See 2 Ne. 33: 11-14). It was the encounter with Sherem which took place as Jacob was an elderly man that caused Jacob to add further to his already completed book. The Sherem encounter ends with verse 23. If Jacob left the metal record at that point, and preserved his writing on other materials without ever returning to etch his final conclusion, then Enos would have been the one responsible for selecting and etching the remaining verses, including this one. That would also explain the rather eclectic and disorderly concluding verses of Jacob's 7th Chapter, which

following: "And it came to pass that many means were devised to reclaim and restore the Lamanites to the knowledge of the truth; but it all was vain, for they delighted in wars and bloodshed, and they had an eternal hatred against us, their brethren. And they sought by the power of their arms to destroy us continually." (Jacob 7: 24.) His father's decidedly negative attitude toward the Lamanites is mirrored in the things Enos says about them.[43] Yet the "many long strugglings" is followed by calling them "my brethren, the Lamanites." Enos is struggling to accept the ultimate end of his people, the triumph of the Lamanites, and the final conversion of the Lamanites to the faith of the Nephites. This would be many generations in the future. This is the destiny shown in vision to Nephi, foretold by Nephi on these same Small Plates on which Enos was writing, and which Enos finally came to accept.

The result of these many long strugglings was the extension of charity to another concentric circle outside Enos. Now he not only feels the charitable love of Christ for his own immediate brethren, but it has worked its way to bring him also to accept and see even

-----

differs markedly from the order and purposefulness of all his prior words.

[43]See Enos 1: 14: "For at the present our strugglings were vain in restoring them to the true faith. And they swore in their wrath that, if it were possible, they would destroy our records and us, and also all the traditions of our fathers." Also verse 20: "And I bear record that the people of Nephi did seek diligently to restore the Lamanites unto the true faith in God. But our labors were vain; their hatred was fixed, and they were led by their evil nature that they became wild, and ferocious, and a blood-thirsty people, full of idolatry and filthiness; feeding upon beasts of prey; dwelling in tents, and wandering about in the wilderness with a short skin girdle about their loins and their heads shaven; and their skill was in the bow, and in the cimeter, and the ax. And many of them did eat nothing save it was raw meat; and they were continually seeking to destroy us."

his enemies as his "brethren." Enos is becoming Christlike. He is following his Master. Enos' Lord would endure the brutality of the Roman abuse and while being nailed by them to the cross "then said Jesus, Father, forgive them; for they know not what they do." (Luke 23: 34.) Despair turns to triumph as anyone begins to accept and trust in God's wisdom. Enos may have endured many long strugglings to get there, but he did arrive. Enos is announcing his own triumph as he refers to these enemies of his people as his brethren!

This is a poignant moment in the record of a real person confronting real personal difficulties. This is not a work of fiction by a backwoods youth. Enos has put on display in a record composed by a fully mature prophet his broken heart and contrite spirit. We are seeing here the fullness of the Gospel of Jesus Christ. Joseph Smith may have translated this record, but he certainly did not have the wisdom or experience at that point in his life to have composed it.

Chapter 6

ASK WHAT YOU WILL

rom time to time we catch a glimpse in the scriptures of something which is most sacred. These events are never fully explained, but they are preserved so those who know what is happening can see the pattern. In the case of Solomon, on the day of the dedication of the Temple by Solomon we find one of these events recorded in these words: "In that night did God appear unto Solomon, and said unto him, Ask what I shall give thee." (2 Chron. 1: 7.)

In another account we read this: "And it came to pass when Jesus had said these words, he spake unto his disciples, one by one, saying unto them: What is it that ye desire of me, after that I am gone to the Father?" (3 Ne. 28: 1.) Christ refers to having asked this same question of His Twelve in Jerusalem: "And when he had spoken unto them, he turned himself unto the three, and said unto them: What will ye that I should do unto you, when I am gone unto the Father? And they sorrowed in their hearts, for they durst not speak unto him the thing which they desired. And he said unto them: Behold, I know your thoughts, and *ye have desired the thing which John, my beloved, who was with me in my ministry, before that I was lifted up by the Jews, desired of me.*" (*Id.*, v. 4-6, emphasis added.) This is further explained in D&C 7, where we read: "And for this cause the Lord said unto Peter: If I will that he tarry till I come, what is that to thee? For he desired of me that he might bring souls unto me, but thou desiredst that thou mightest speedily come unto me in my kingdom. I say unto thee, Peter, this was a good desire; but my beloved has desired that he might do more, or a greater work yet among men than what he has before done." (Verses 4-5.) All these were given a similar opportunity to ask for anything from the Lord.

These occasions occur in the Old Testament, New Testament and in the Book of Mormon where Christ has invited some to request anything they may desire from Him. The descriptions suggest whatever those invited individuals may ask He will grant to them. Although the setting is not explained, we know there are those to whom He has offered this profound opportunity. We know Solomon asked for wisdom. John and the Three Nephites asked to linger here among us. Nine of the Twelve in the Americas and ten of the Twelve in Jerusalem asked to "come speedily" to Christ in His kingdom. Apparently Moses and Elijah asked to carry on assignments which took them to heaven without tasting of death. So the question arises as to why this opportunity is given to some from time to time. It should be apparent from what we are now reading about Enos, that when the Lord personally conducts the ordinance of making a man's calling and election sure, as a part of the rite the Lord invites the man to ask anything he may desire of the Lord. This invitation shows not only the trust between the Lord and the man, but confirms the trustworthiness of the man. Only someone who would never misplace such trust would be extended such an offer.

It is safe to conclude anyone who arrives at this point enters

into a wholly different kind of relationship with the Lord. They
become part of a new brotherhood, in which they are able with
Christ to say "Abba, Father."[44] This kind of trusting relationship
cannot occur unless the person entering into it is a trustworthy,
obedient[45] companion.

As we have seen, the responses to the Lord's offer include a
request for wisdom, requests to remain here to continue to minister
to mortals, and requests to enter speedily into Christ's Kingdom.
None of these requests are really what they seem. Solomon's
request for wisdom was not fulfilled until very late in his lifetime.
Early when he proposed to divide the baby (1 Kings 3: 16-28) and
thereby identified the true mother, he was still not in possession of
wisdom. God's obligation to give wisdom extended well beyond
mere mortal cleverness. Solomon was given worldly success and
power, which in turn yielded failures that produced wisdom. "Of
the nations concerning which the Lord said unto the children of
Israel, Ye shall not go in to them, neither shall they come in unto
you: for surely they will turn away your heart after their gods:

---

[44]See Rom. 8: 15 and Gal. 4: 6. Joseph Smith referred to these
kinds of people briefly in this comment: "'Now,' says God, when He
visited Moses in the bush, (Moses was a stammering sort of a boy like me)
God said, 'Thou shalt be a God unto the children of Israel.' God said,
'Thou shalt be a God unto Aaron, and he shall be thy spokesman.' I
believe those Gods that God reveals as Gods to be sons of God, and all
can cry, 'Abba, Father!' Sons of God who exalt themselves to be Gods,
even from before the foundation of the world, and are the only Gods I
have a reverence for. (*TPJS*, p. 375.) So there are others who can cry
"Abba, Father" as a result of their being "begotten" by God, as referred
to in Psalms 2: 7.

[45]As used here, the word "obedient" refers to the relationship with
God; and not necessarily the way in which others may perceive them. Such
people must be fearless toward the desires of their fellow men, willing to
endure being misunderstood or rejected. Their relationship with and
fidelity to the Lord would be paramount.

Solomon clave unto these in love. And he had seven hundred wives, princesses, and three hundred concubines: and his wives turned away his heart. For it came to pass, when Solomon was old, that his wives turned away his heart after other gods: and his heart was not perfect with the Lord his God… For Solomon went after Ashtoreth the goddess of the Zidonians, and after Milcom the abomination of the Ammonites. And Solomon did evil in the sight of the Lord, and went not fully after the Lord… Then did Solomon build an high place for Chemosh, the abomination of Moab, in the hill that is before Jerusalem, and for Molech, the abomination of the children of Ammon. And likewise did he for all his strange wives, which burnt incense and sacrificed unto their gods. And the Lord was angry with Solomon, because his heart was turned from the Lord God of Israel, which had appeared unto him twice, And had commanded him concerning this thing, that he should not go after other gods: but he kept not that which the Lord commanded. Wherefore the Lord said unto Solomon, Forasmuch as this is done of thee, and thou hast not kept my covenant and my statutes, which I have commanded thee, I will surely rend the kingdom from thee, and will give it to thy servant." (1 Kings 11: 2-11.) Query which "kingdom" is meant by the Lord in this statement? Was it limited to the Kingdom of Israel, or did it also include another kingdom forfeited hereafter? How far does one fall who has had the Lord "appear unto him twice" and then afterwards they "keep not the commandments which the Lord commanded them?" When Solomon was put through judgment for his failure, and informed of the Lord's disappointment with him, he finally understood and wrote: "Let us hear the conclusion of the whole matter: Fear God, and keep his commandments: for this is the whole duty of man. For God shall bring every work into judgment, with every secret thing,

whether it be good, or whether it be evil." (Ecc. 12: 13-14.)
Solomon did learn wisdom. But it was not a gift without a price. It
came through experience, failure, forfeiture, repentance and he
hoped, forgiveness. His life of success was summarized by him:
"Vanity of vanities, saith the preacher; all is vanity." (*Id.*, v. 8.)
Wisdom can be a bitter thing. By the end of his life and in the time
following it, by bitter reflection Solomon did obtain what he asked
to receive. He has shared his wisdom with us so we may learn
wisdom without experiencing similar personal bitterness.

As to the continuing mortal ministries, we have a fuller
explanation in D&C Section 7.[46] We know John appeared with
Peter and James to restore Melchizedek Priesthood to Joseph and
Oliver. (See JS-H 1: 72 and D&C 128: 20.) The scriptures inform us
John has been a "minister for those who shall be heirs of salvation
who dwell on the earth." John has, no doubt, been a witness to
those "heirs of salvation" even if such people are among "those
which I [the Lord] have reserved unto myself, holy men that ye

---

[46]"And the Lord said unto me: John, my beloved, what desirest
thou? For if you shall ask what you will, it shall be granted unto you. And
I said unto him: Lord, give unto me power over death, that I may live and
bring souls unto thee. And the Lord said unto me: Verily, verily, I say
unto thee, because thou desirest this thou shalt tarry until I come in my
glory, and shalt prophesy before nations, kindreds, tongues and people.
And for this cause the Lord said unto Peter: If I will that he tarry till I
come, what is that to thee? For he desired of me that he might bring souls
unto me, but thou desiredst that thou mightest speedily come unto me in
my kingdom. I say unto thee, Peter, this was a good desire; but my
beloved has desired that he might do more, or a greater work yet among
men than what he has before done. Yea, he has undertaken a greater
work; therefore I will make him as flaming fire and a ministering angel; he
shall minister for those who shall be heirs of salvation who dwell on the
earth. And I will make thee to minister for him and for thy brother James;
and unto you three I will give this power and the keys of this ministry
until I come. Verily I say unto you, ye shall both have according to your
desires, for ye both joy in that which ye have desired." (D&C 7: 1-8.)

know not of." (D&C 49: 8.) John's continuing ministry may be undisclosed to us at present, but our ignorance does not limit his service.

The final known request, to "come speedily" into Christ's kingdom is also an interesting desire. It does not mean die and go to the Spirit World, as set out in Section 138. "For the dead had looked upon the long absence of their spirits from their bodies as a bondage." (D&C 138: 50.) They were not asking to go into bondage. Rather, they asked the Lord: "We desire that after we have lived unto the age of man, that our ministry, wherein thou hast called us, may have an end, that we may speedily *come unto thee in thy kingdom.*" (3 Ne. 28: 2, emphasis added.) They asked to bypass the Spirit World altogether. They wanted to come to Christ, and live in His kingdom, which necessarily required them to be resurrected. We know there are those who have already inherited a Celestial Glory, and who presently sit upon thrones.[47] These disciples wanted to join them.

Each of these three responses to the Lord's offer are profound. They contrast, however, with Enos' response. Enos took considerable time to reflect before concluding to ask the Lord to benefit his enemies. Enos records:

> 12 And it came to pass that after I had prayed and labored with all diligence, the Lord said unto me: I will grant unto thee according to thy desires, because of thy faith.

---

[47]See D&C 132: 29: "Abraham received all things, whatsoever he received, by revelation and commandment, by my word, saith the Lord, and hath entered into his exaltation and sitteth upon his throne." Also verse 37: "Isaac also and Jacob did none other things than that which they were commanded; and because they did none other things than that which they were commanded, they have entered into their exaltation, according to the promises, and sit upon thrones, and are not angels but are gods."

Remember from the prior Chapter that Enos had previously endured many long struggles inside himself to come to a conclusion about what to ask. He does not make a perfunctory request. Enos could have asked for anything. It is all the more remarkable that Enos, when put to the test, decided to make a request for the benefit of his enemies, now his "brethren." The depth of Enos' humility is almost unfathomable. He asks nothing for himself; not wisdom, long life, a continuing mortal ministry, nor even to come speedily into the Lord's kingdom. Instead he asks the Lord to bless those who have rejected him, his people and his people's faith in Christ. We are reading a sacred account written by a man who followed Christ. We have surely come to holy ground as we are allowed this view into the relationship between Enos and his Lord. It is no wonder the Lord will later comment on Enos' great faith.

Enos continues:

> 13 And now behold, this was the desire which I desired of him--that if it should so be, that my people, the Nephites, should fall into transgression, and by any means be destroyed, and the Lamanites should not be destroyed, that the Lord God would preserve a record of my people, the Nephites; even if it so be by the power of his holy arm, that it might be brought forth at some future day unto the Lamanites, that, perhaps, they might be brought unto salvation[.]

This is what Nephi saw in vision. This is what he carved onto the Small Plates of Nephi (on which Enos was now writing). With these words Enos is accepting the prophecy of Nephi, and more likely also accepting the things which his "many long struggling" led him to realize.

Nephi knew his descendants would fail in their faith, be destroyed by the Lamanites, and that the Lamanites would also lose the true faith.[48] Nephi also wrote that the record or testimony of the Nephites would be restored to the Lamanites at some future time.[49]

---

[48]For example see Nephi's prophetic description of the Lamanite triumph and Nephite destruction in 1 Ne. 12: 14-19: "And the angel said unto me: Behold thy seed, and also the seed of thy brethren. And it came to pass that I looked and beheld the people of my seed gathered together in multitudes against the seed of my brethren; and they were gathered together to battle. And the angel spake unto me, saying: Behold the fountain of filthy water which thy father saw; yea, even the river of which he spake; and the depths thereof are the depths of hell. And the mists of darkness are the temptations of the devil, which blindeth the eyes, and hardeneth the hearts of the children of men, and leadeth them away into broad roads, that they perish and are lost. And the large and spacious building, which thy father saw, is vain imaginations and the pride of the children of men. And a great and a terrible gulf divideth them; yea, even the word of the justice of the Eternal God, and the Messiah who is the Lamb of God, of whom the Holy Ghost beareth record, from the beginning of the world until this time, and from this time henceforth and forever. And while the angel spake these words, *I beheld and saw that the seed of my brethren did contend against my seed,* according to the word of the angel; and *because of the pride of my seed, and the temptations of the devil, I beheld that the seed of my brethren did overpower the people of my seed.*" (Emphasis added.)

[49]1 Ne. 13: 35-41: "For, behold, saith the Lamb: *I will manifest myself unto thy seed,* that they shall write many things which I shall minister unto them, which shall be plain and precious; and *after thy seed shall be destroyed, and dwindle in unbelief, and also the seed of thy brethren, behold, these things shall be hid up, to come forth unto the Gentiles,* by the gift and power of the Lamb. And *in them shall be written my gospel,* saith the Lamb, and my rock and my salvation. And blessed are they who shall seek to bring forth my Zion at that day, for they shall have the gift and the power of the Holy Ghost; and if they endure unto the end they shall be lifted up at the last day, and shall be saved in the everlasting kingdom of the Lamb; and whoso shall publish peace, yea, tidings of great joy, how beautiful upon the mountains shall they be. And it came to pass that I beheld the remnant of the seed of my brethren, and also the book of the Lamb of God, which had proceeded forth from the mouth of the Jew, that it came forth from the Gentiles unto the remnant of the seed of my brethren. And after it had come forth unto them *I beheld other books, which came forth by the power of the Lamb, from the Gentiles unto them, unto the convincing of the Gentiles and the remnant of the seed of my brethren, and also the Jews who were*

Given that Nephi wrote these things on the same plates on which Enos was now writing, the question arises as to why Enos puts his wording so tentative. He does not come right out and repeat what Nephi had written. Instead he makes this future uncertain. He writes: "[I]f it should so be, that my people, the Nephites, should fall into transgression, and by any means..." He knew this was going to happen. It is already prophesied in the very plates on which he was etching his own record. Given this, we should consider *why* he uses tentative language rather than definite language to describe this already known future. It was not because he was unaware of his people's fate. Nor was it due to a lack of faith on his part. Rather, since Enos would have been given the sealing power as a part of having his calling and election made sure,[50] he would have been

---

scattered upon all the face of the earth, that the records of the prophets and of the twelve apostles of the Lamb are true. And the angel spake unto me, saying: *These last records, which thou hast seen among the Gentiles, shall establish the truth of the first, which are of the twelve apostles of the Lamb,* and shall make known the plain and precious things which have been taken away from them; and shall make known to all kindreds, tongues, and people, that the Lamb of God is the Son of the Eternal Father, and the Savior of the world; and that all men must come unto him, or they cannot be saved. And they must come according to the words which shall be established by the mouth of the Lamb; and *the words of the Lamb shall be made known in the records of thy seed,* as well as in the records of the twelve apostles of the Lamb; wherefore they both shall be established in one; for there is one God and one Shepherd over all the earth." (Emphasis added.)

[50]The Church holds the sealing power as a part of the restoration of all things. Otherwise the Church could not discharge its responsibilities given to her. However, when a man is made a king and priest to the Most High God, he also necessarily must have sealing power to establish his kingdom. For the Church, this power is general, and exercised throughout the world as a part of its mission. For the man, it is given him for the limited purpose of saving his family or kingdom. Joseph commented on three degrees of priesthood: Aaronic, Melchizedek and Patriarchal. We read in *TPJS* p. 323: "The **Melchizedek Priesthood** holds the right from the eternal God, and not by descent from father and mother; and that

cautious about how he stated in his sacred writings his descendants' fate. Remember that once someone has been given the power to bind the Lord, the Lord has committed Himself to vindicate the words of such a servant.[51] Enos' use of tentative language on something which has already been prophesied by Nephi is one of the confirming evidences that Enos has been given the sealing power (and correspondingly had his calling and election made sure). He did not want anything he said or wrote to bind the Lord to this unwanted outcome. Although he could accept this future and even call the enemy victors over his descendants his "brethren," he did not want to own any part of the responsibility for this fate.

Enos gives a display of the kind of character traits required for these most sacred things. People involved in such rites are able to honor sacred things and to handle with profound care the trust shown by the Lord. Enos shows us what we should all be trying to become. He has become sacred space in his very body, a Temple of

---

priesthood is as eternal as God Himself, having neither beginning of days nor end of life. The 2nd Priesthood is **Patriarchal authority**. Go to and finish the temple, and God will fill it with power, and you will then receive more knowledge concerning this priesthood. The 3rd is what is called the **Levitical Priesthood**, consisting of priests to administer in outward ordinances, made without an oath; but the Priesthood of Melchizedek is by an oath and covenant." (Emphasis added.) The Church possesses and administers all three. Those who have their callings and election made sure also hold all three.

[51]See D&C 1: 38: "What I the Lord have spoken, I have spoken, and I excuse not myself; and though the heavens and the earth pass away, my word shall not pass away, but shall all be fulfilled, *whether by mine own voice or by the voice of my servants, it is the same.*" (Emphasis added.) In the case of someone holding sealing power, therefore, words must be used with caution. Only the cautious would ever qualify. We discuss this further in the final Chapter of this book

God.[52] He has become the place where the infinite and eternal touches the finite and mortal.

Enos continues:

> 14 For at the present our strugglings were vain in restoring them to the true faith. And they swore in their wrath that, if it were possible, they would destroy our records and us, and also all the traditions of our fathers.

We find the same word used to describe both Enos' personal conflict in accepting the Lamanite future triumph and the Nephite difficulties in converting the Lamanites. Both involved "strug- glings."

Interestingly, the Lamanite ambition involved destroying first and foremost the Nephite "records." These records preserved the Nephite memory of what was sacred.[53] The Lamanites feared and resented this power to recall accurately the sacred learning of ages passed.

Secondly, the Lamanites wanted to destroy the Nephites. This did not involve genocide because in the vernacular of the Book of Mormon to "destroy" did not mean annihilate. It merely meant to end their organized existence, or to terminate their government, deprive them of a separate land and end their cultural dominance. We read in 2 Ne. 25: 9: "And as one generation hath been destroyed among the Jews because of iniquity, even so have they been destroyed from generation to generation according to their

---

[52]See e.g., 1 Cor 3: 16: "Know ye not that ye are the temple of God, and that the Spirit of God dwelleth in you?"

[53]Laban was slain in order to obtain the brass plates. See 1 Ne. 4: 13: "Behold the Lord slayeth the wicked to bring forth his righteous purposes. It is better that one man should perish than that a nation should dwindle and perish in unbelief."

iniquities; and never hath any of them been destroyed save it were foretold them by the prophets of the Lord." Although some Jews were killed in the process, the real "destruction" of the Jews was the loss of their homeland, loss of their government, loss of their self-determination and loss of their individuality as a distinct culture for generations. It is in this sense the Lamanites sought to destroy the Nephites.

Finally, they sought to destroy the Nephite traditions. As used here, they sought to end the Nephite religious traditions. By the time of Enos' writing, the Lamanites had their own religious traditions and they were nothing like the Nephite faith. Enos will give us a glimpse inside that new and deviant religious form adopted by the Lamanites. We will see that a little further on in this book.

The traditions, government and records of the Nephites were all linked together. Their peoplehood reckoned from the sacred texts they owned, followed and kept. It is clear the Lamanites understood this relationship and therefore specifically targeted the records for destruction.

Enos knew the records they were keeping would add to the knowledge any reader already had of God. Therefore, Enos wanted to have these Nephite records come to the attention of a worthy people at some future day. He continues:

> 15 Wherefore, I knowing that the Lord God was able to preserve our records, I cried unto him continually, for he had said unto me: Whatsoever thing ye shall ask in faith, believing that ye shall receive in the name of Christ, ye shall receive it.
> 16 And I had faith, and I did cry unto God that he would preserve the records; and he covenanted with me that he would bring them forth unto the Lamanites in his own due time.

It is significant Enos mentions a "covenant" involving the records.

God "keepeth covenant" with us. (See e.g., D&C 109: 1.) We discussed that before, but note again here that Enos knew the Lord takes His covenants most seriously. Therefore any covenant to preserve these records would be fulfilled.

Enos' description again is stated in words which suggest the passing of time. When he writes: "I cried unto him continually" it does not mean a single encounter or petition. It suggests Enos worked on this covenant for some extended period before obtaining the results he desired.

We should not expect our own struggles to be any less. Too often we quickly abandon a petition to God because we do not get the immediate results we want. We are impatient. That is a mistake when dealing with a Lord who wants to teach all His children the virtue of patience. He reminds us repeatedly in the scriptures we need to be patient. (See e.g., Mosiah 3: 19; Alma 13: 28; Alma 17: 11; Alma 20: 29; Alma 26: 28; D&C 6: 1; D&C 9: 3; D&C 11: 19; D&C 24: 8; and D&C 31: 9 among many others.)

It would be a mistake to think Enos had it easier than the rest of us. He accomplished what he did against the very same difficulties each one of us must confront and overcome. There are no exemptions granted to anyone. When we find a record as Enos has left us, we should all rejoice that the path has been successfully trodden by another. There is hope for us all.

The promise of delivering the records to the Lamanites is tied to the "own due time" of the Lord. In this context the "time" refers to the arrival of a prepared people who will accept the records. As it turns out that event is still future. We are working toward it, but have not seen it and will not see it until the sealed portion of the Book of Mormon is published.

The Lord set in motion the fulfillment of the covenant with

Joseph Smith. Getting the plates to Joseph, having the plates translated and printed, building an infrastructure to publish the book across the world in many languages, establishing the Church, gathering a people, and finally putting in motion a missionary army to flood the world were necessary preconditions to the covenant actually being completed. It will be completed when the Lamanites assume their responsibilities within the Church itself. As the times of the Gentiles end, and they are swept away from the Americas, the Lamanites will replace the Gentiles and assume responsibility for governing at last. Christ Himself foretold how the corrupt Gentiles occupying this land will be swept away: "Then shall ye, who are a remnant of the house of Jacob, go forth among them; and ye shall be in the midst of them who shall be many; and ye shall be among them as a lion among the beasts of the forest, and as a young lion among the flocks of sheep, who, if he goeth through both treadeth down and teareth in pieces, and none can deliver." (3 Ne. 20: 16.) There are now forces currently in motion which could fulfill this treading down and tearing in pieces.

This passing of the Gentiles will not be limited to the remnant taking vengeance. The Lord will also participate: "But, behold, I say unto you that before this great day shall come the sun shall be darkened, and the moon shall be turned into blood, and the stars shall fall from heaven, and there shall be greater signs in heaven above and in the earth beneath; And there shall be weeping and wailing among the hosts of men; And there shall be a great hailstorm sent forth to destroy the crops of the earth. And it shall come to pass, because of the wickedness of the world, that I will take vengeance upon the wicked, for they will not repent; for the cup of mine indignation is full; for behold, my blood shall not cleanse them if they hear me not. Wherefore, I the Lord God will send forth flies upon the face of the earth, which shall take hold of the inhabitants thereof, and shall eat their flesh, and shall cause maggots to come in upon them; And their tongues shall be stayed that they shall not utter against me; and their flesh shall fall from off their bones, and their eyes from their sockets; And it shall come to pass that the beasts of the forest and the fowls of the air shall devour them up. And the great and abominable church, which is the whore of all the earth, shall be cast down by devouring fire, according as it is spoken by the mouth of Ezekiel the prophet, who spoke of these things, which have not come to pass but surely must, as I live, for abominations shall not reign." (D&C 29: 14-21.) While not a pleasant picture, it produces a necessary result. The earth, and in particular the Americas, are intended to be sacred. It is the destiny of this land to be occupied by people who live worthily upon it. At present the earth is full of spiritual pollutions and uncleanness. The Lord guarantees us it will not continue uncorrected. Cleansing the Americas of gross wickedness will require the Gentiles to be swept away. Their time is now passing, as lowering birth rates and shifting demographic figures unmistakenly show.

We read, too: "Behold, vengeance cometh speedily upon the inhabitants of the earth, a day of wrath, a day of burning, a day of desolation, of weeping, of mourning, and of lamentation; and as a whirlwind it shall come upon all the face of the earth, saith the Lord. And upon my house shall it begin, and from my house shall it go forth, saith the Lord; First among those among you, saith the Lord, who have professed to know my name and have not known me, and have blasphemed against me in the midst of my house, saith the Lord." (D&C 112: 24-26.) Latter-day Saints will be corrected by the leading edge of the Lord's wrath. From those who claim to have much, much is required. Since the Saints claim to know the Lord He will hold them to the standard of actually knowing Him.

The "due time of the Lord" will involve many events which will refine and prepare people to receive power through sacred Priestly rites so they may be preserved in the plagues to come. It would be best if those who now have the Gospel took it more seriously. But if not, we have the promise they will be swept away and replaced by others who will.

Chapter 7

THE FAITH OF ENOS/
THE FAITH OF THE LAMANITES

*E*nos added next to his record:

> 17 And I, Enos, knew it would be according to the covenant which he had made; wherefore my soul did rest.

This is another confirmation that Enos' relationship with the Lord is based on a covenant. He knew the Lord was fully committed to keeping the covenant between them. Therefore, as to such an obligation Enos could "rest." He needn't worry. There is no need for further concern because when the Lord has spoken it, it will happen.

This leads to the next statement in Enos' record:

> 18 And the Lord said unto me: Thy fathers have also required of me this thing; and it shall be done unto them according to their faith; for their faith was like unto thine.

It is as though the Lord had all the past generations in mind when he, in effect, said to Enos: "Oh, yes, you are asking me what many others before you have asked me. I have already made this promise, and I have intended to bring this to pass for some time now." Here we learn that Enos' inspired request was consistent with the Lord's prior commitment to the "fathers."

This statement becomes more significant as we contemplate the unidentified "fathers." Who are the "fathers" mentioned in this verse? Who previously has "required" this promise toward the Lamanites? Some are obvious. Others are less so. Among the more obvious candidates is Jacob, Enos' immediate father. Jacob reiterated the allegory of Zenos. Zenos' allegory has clear reference to the latter-day restoration of a branch of Israel in this most desirable part of the vineyard. (See Jacob 5: 43-46, 54-74.)

Nephi would also be one of the "fathers" who had the Lord's covenant to restore the Lamanites. Nephi wrote prophetically, promising the latter-day restoration of the record he and his descendants would write. The record would be of great value to these separated descendants of Israel.[54] Although Lehi's record was lost as a part of the 116 pages Martin Harris caused to be forfeited, no doubt Lehi would be among the "fathers" to whom the promise was made as well. We would know that if Lehi's record was available.

There are other more distant "fathers" who would undoubtedly be included as well. For example Joseph of Egypt prophesied about a descendant (Joseph Smith) who would restore records in the last days.[55] His father, Jacob or Israel, prophesied of Joseph's descen-

---

[54]See e.g., 2 Ne. 28: 1-2: "And now, behold, my brethren, I have spoken unto you, according as the Spirit hath constrained me; wherefore, I know that they must surely come to pass. And the things which shall be written out of the book shall be of great worth unto the children of men, and especially unto our seed, which is a remnant of the house of Israel."

[55]See e.g., 2 Ne. 3: 6-7: " For Joseph truly testified, saying: A seer shall the Lord my God raise up, who shall be a choice seer unto the fruit

dants in the patriarchal blessing found in Genesis, Chapter 49.[56] These descendants would spread over the wall of the well – or in other words would spread beyond a body of water. They would be among those Israelites scattered to the "isles of the sea." (Isa. 24: 15.) The Nephites and Lamanites were on an isle of the sea.[57] Therefore both Jacob and Isaiah are likely among the "fathers" with whom the Lord made a prior covenant.

Going all the way back to the beginning of mankind, we read this about father Adam: "Three years previous to the death of Adam, he called Seth, Enos, Cainan, Mahalaleel, Jared, Enoch, and Methuselah, who were all high priests, with the residue of his posterity who were righteous, into the valley of Adam-ondi-Ahman, and there bestowed upon them his last blessing. And the Lord

---

of my loins. Yea, Joseph truly said: Thus saith the Lord unto me: A choice seer will I raise up out of the fruit of thy loins; and he shall be esteemed highly among the fruit of thy loins. And unto him will I give commandment that he shall do a work for the fruit of thy loins, his brethren, which shall be of great worth unto them, even to the bringing of them to the knowledge of the covenants which I have made with thy fathers."

[56]"Joseph is a fruitful bough, even a fruitful bough by a well; whose branches run over the wall: The archers have sorely grieved him, and shot at him, and hated him: But his bow abode in strength, and the arms of his hands were made strong by the hands of the mighty God of Jacob; (from thence is the shepherd, the stone of Israel:) Even by the God of thy father, who shall help thee; and by the Almighty, who shall bless thee with blessings of heaven above, blessings of the deep that lieth under, blessings of the breasts, and of the womb: The blessings of thy father have prevailed above the blessings of my progenitors unto the utmost bound of the everlasting hills: they shall be on the head of Joseph, and on the crown of the head of him that was separate from his brethren." (Gen. 49: 22-26.)

[57]2 Ne. 10: 20: "[W]e have been led to a better land, for the Lord has made the sea our path, and we are upon an isle of the sea."

appeared unto them, and they rose up and blessed Adam, and called him Michael, the prince, the archangel. And the Lord administered comfort unto Adam, and said unto him: I have set thee to be at the head; a multitude of nations shall come of thee, and thou art a prince over them forever. And Adam stood up in the midst of the congregation; and, notwithstanding he was bowed down with age, *being full of the Holy Ghost, predicted whatsoever should befall his posterity unto the latest generation.* These things were all written in the book of Enoch, and are to be testified of in due time." (D&C 107: 53-57, emphasis added.) When Adam spoke these things he held priesthood, and spoke by the power of the Holy Ghost. These words were authorized by God and binding upon the Lord. Adam's prophecy is among those words He intends to fulfill and "not excuse." Adam's prophetic words about all his descendants would have included the Lamanites and their ultimate restoration to the Gospel in the latter-days. As a result, we should include Adam in the "fathers" who have required the Lord to restore the Gospel to the Lamanites in the last days.

There are others. However, we have enough of a list to put into context Enos' comments. Enos is told by the Lord: "their faith was like unto thine." The Lord knew all these fathers. He had appeared unto many - possibly all - of them. He knew the covenants He had entered into with each of them, and He compares the "faith" of Enos to the "faith" of Adam, Abraham, Israel, Joseph, Lehi, Nephi, and Jacob, among many others. It is wonderful to contemplate this. We are reading from Enos a record of a man whom the Lord considered to be equal in faith to Adam and Abraham.

Ancient luminaries like Adam or Abraham can seem very distant. Not just in time, but also distant in their mortal spiritual development. Enos, by comparison, does not seem quite as distant.

His book seems meek, in the truest sense of the word. He writes as if he were like the rest of us. Writers like Enos bring us hope, not discouragement. We relate to them and are not tempted to hold an overly inflated view of them.

Meekness means a person voluntarily restrains themselves and uses the absolute minimum control or authority over others. It is related to humility. Humility is voluntary submission to the control or power of God; or in other words, obedience. Meekness affects a person's relationship with their fellow man. There is nothing showy or attention-grabbing about the meek. Instead, they are content to know they have a relationship and power with God. Unless God requires something to be done, or revealed, the meek do not voluntarily put this authority on display. Moses was criticized by Aaron, his brother, and Miriam, his sister[58] because they were discontent over an Ethiopian wife.[59] Left to himself, Moses would have endured the criticism with patience. He did not expect to be beyond criticism. The record informs us: "Now the man Moses was very meek, above all the men which were upon the face of the earth." (Num 12: 3.) Therefore he did not feel himself above criticism from anyone, even his closest associates.

Moses had stood in the presence of God. He had, with the Lord's power, subdued the great Pharaoh and his armies. He was used by God to part a sea, save the children of Israel, and perform miracles which even distant nations would notice. He was the unquestioned leader of a nation, whose standing was next to God

[58]Num 26: 59: "And the name of Amram's wife was Jochebed, the daughter of Levi, whom her mother bare to Levi in Egypt: and she bare unto Amram Aaron and Moses, and Miriam their sister."

[59]Num 12: 1: "And Miriam and Aaron spake against Moses because of the Ethiopian woman whom he had married: for he had married an Ethiopian woman."

in the eyes of the people. Yet, when criticized by his brother and sister, he did nothing to defend himself. The power which the Lord had entrusted to him would not be used to justify his actions, unless the Lord required it of him.[60] Meekness does not vaunt itself, and does not seek to avoid criticism. The meek never confuse their personal pride with the Lord's will or work. They never believe themselves to be more than a poor instrument in the hands of an Almighty God. They never confuse magnifying a calling with their responsibility to use only meekness, love unfeigned, pure knowledge and persuasion. For such individuals the service they render supercedes any need for personal recognition. Even though they may occupy a position of honor, they do not tolerate personal praise or devotion to themselves. Such men use their authority to honor God, and never themselves. We find very few meek men. Enos was one.

Enos wrote a meek book. It is measured, deliberate and understated. It contains profound truths about the most sacred things which can be written by a man. But it does not force itself into notice. His record can be read by the spiritually blind without ever noticing the significance of what he records. The statement about the quality of Enos' faith is both meek and understated. It is the Lord who makes the comparison. Enos reports it only in

---

[60]In this instance, the Lord took offense at Aaron's and Miriam's murmuring, and did something about it. The Lord personally rebuked both of them, and struck Miriam with leprosy. Moses, in turn, took compassion on her and asked the Lord to heal Miriam. She was healed, but excluded from the Camp of Israel for a week because of her temporary ceremonial uncleanness. (See Numbers 12: 5-15.) Moses did not take offense, and when the Lord rebuked his critics he petitioned on their behalf. Rather than being thin-skinned, defensive or jealous to avoid criticism and receive only praise, Moses was "very meek, above all the men which were upon the face of the earth." It is one of the reasons he was among the greatest of prophets.

passing. The careful student will be struck with wonder at the Lord's comparison of this man with the covenantal fathers, which include some of the greatest patriarchs of all history.

He continues:

> 19 And now it came to pass that I, Enos, went about among the people of Nephi, prophesying of things to come, and testifying of the things which I had heard and seen.

Enos resumes his teaching. He "went about among the people of Nephi." He did not set himself apart. He did not ask people to come to him. He went among them. He was not distant or aloof. His ministry was close and personal; "among" the people he was asked to teach.

Teachers cannot really teach from a distance. They can evoke acclaim, respect and acquire notoriety from a distance. They can even become celebrities. But to be an effective teacher Enos had to go meet face to face. Even the Lord does this. To Moses, the Lord explained how He would minister to His followers: "With him will I speak mouth to mouth, even apparently, and not in dark speeches; and the similitude of the Lord shall he behold[.]" (Num. 12: 8.) Moroni also wrote: "And then shall ye know that I have seen Jesus, and that he hath talked with me face to face, and that he told me in plain humility, even as a man telleth another in mine own language, concerning these things[.]" (Ether 12: 39.) With respect to the Brother of Jared it is recorded: "Wherefore, ... he could not be kept from within the veil; therefore he saw Jesus; and he did minister unto him." (Ether 3: 20.) At the dedication of the Kirtland Temple the Lord declared: "Yea, I will appear unto my servants, and speak unto them with mine own voice, if my people will keep my commandments, and do not pollute this holy house." (D&C 110: 8.)

In His mortal ministry, Christ ministered directly to the crowds who would hear Him. There are many other examples, but these are enough to show how the Lord continues to minister personally to His followers. Enos is imitating the Lord when he ministered "among the people," rather than from a distance. The Lord was not and is not aloof. Neither was Enos. To effectively minister, the personal presence of the one ministering is essential. It will never be otherwise. Enos was not interested in being admired from a distance. Rather he was interested in teaching in person. This is one of the great and relevant points of Enos' record. Those who choose to distance themselves from the Lord's sheep will never be known by the sheep as anything other than an icon.

His ministry consisted of what knew. He could "testify" as a witness of things to come. His prophecy was personal. He knew the truth of his message. Such a personal message required a personal delivery by Enos for it to be effective.

As we have previously pointed out, Enos' experience was not limited to hearing a voice. He saw the Lord. He reconfirms that in this verse. He testified "of the things which I had heard and *seen.*" He could not have included things which he had "seen" unless the Lord showed something to him. Enos, in his meekness, does not force the conclusion upon us, but he does embed it in his message. If we carefully consider his words, we are forced to conclude that Enos' testimony includes a witness of having seen Christ.

Next, Enos gives us a glimpse into the early Lamanite religious practices. These early deviations at the beginning (second generation) would later mutate into the varying faiths on display during the Alma the Younger/Sons of Mosiah missionary era. His record tells us:

> 20 And I bear record that the people of Nephi did

seek diligently to restore the Lamanites unto the
true faith in God. But our labors were vain; their
hatred was fixed, and they were led by their evil
nature that they became wild, and ferocious, and a
blood-thirsty people, full of idolatry and filthiness;
feeding upon beasts of prey; dwelling in tents, and
wandering about in the wilderness with a short skin
girdle about their loins and their heads shaven; and
their skill was in the bow, and in the cimeter, and
the ax. And many of them did eat nothing save it
was raw meat; and they were continually seeking to
destroy us.

The time for the Lamanite conversion to the Gospel was still in
the future. Prophecies about them may have encouraged belief they
would convert in Enos' day. The efforts to accomplish this
conversion were futile. The Lamanite "hatred" of the Nephites
prevented it. The wounded feelings of grandparents had been
successfully transferred to the grandchildren. Missionary work was
not going to succeed.

The Lord in His wisdom knows that it is the nature of most
men that their hatred does not pass from a people for three to four
generations. It is one of the truths we see repeated in modern
revelation.[61] This was too soon for a Lamanite conversion. "[T]heir

---

[61]See e.g., D&C 98: 45-46: "I, the Lord, will avenge thee of thine
enemy an hundred-fold; And upon his children, and upon his children's
children of all them that hate me, unto the third and fourth generation.
And upon his children, and upon his children's children of all them that
hate me, unto the third and fourth generation." D&C 103: 26: "And my
presence shall be with you even in avenging me of mine enemies, unto the
third and fourth generation of them that hate me." D&C 105: 30: "And
after these lands are purchased, I will hold the armies of Israel guiltless in
taking possession of their own lands, which they have previously
purchased with their moneys, and of throwing down the towers of mine
enemies that may be upon them, and scattering their watchmen, and
avenging me of mine enemies unto the third and fourth generation of

hatred was fixed" against the Nephites and the Nephite religion. That is the way it was destined to remain until enough generations had passed for the descendants to be unemotional about the dispute. When animosity drifts into legend, the descendants no longer harbor their hatreds. We read newspaper accounts about the fourth-generation of the Hatfields and McCoys holding reunions together to celebrate their famous feud. That would have been unimaginable even two generations earlier.

He wrote next: "and they were led by their evil nature that they became wild, and ferocious, and a blood-thirsty people[.]" Their "evil nature" refers to their inherited disposition to rebel, not merely their mortality. The desire to rebel had been carried into the extreme of being "wild" and "ferocious" and "blood-thirsty." The extent of this becomes clear as we read on.

The Lamanite position was informed by their apostate religious views. Their behavior reckoned from a core set of beliefs. Enos was giving us a larger view of the Lamanite condition as he described for us how they were: "full of idolatry and filthiness[.]" This behavior was based upon "idolatry," meaning their behavior reflected their beliefs. Their beliefs were idolatrous. And when he describes them as "full of filthiness" he is not speaking about hygiene. He is speaking of their religious practices. The "pollutions" of the Lamanites written of later by Mormon, was speaking of spiritual

---

them that hate me." D&C 124: 50, 52: "And the iniquity and transgression of my holy laws and commandments I will visit upon the heads of those who hindered my work, unto the third and fourth generation, so long as they repent not, and hate me, saith the Lord God… And I will answer judgment, wrath, and indignation, wailing, and anguish, and gnashing of teeth upon their heads, unto the third and fourth generation, so long as they repent not, and hate me, saith the Lord your God." Persecution and bitterness do not depart until after three to four generations have passed. The apostates from the Church not only leave, they take their children and grandchildren with them.

degeneracy, not environmental conditions. They failed to follow the required rites to become spiritually pure, and as a result they were impure, or "filthy" under Nephite spiritual standards.

By referring to the issue of the Lamanite idolatry and spiritual filthiness, Enos puts a context to the words which follow. Everything he lists thereafter should be read as examples of the benighted spiritual condition of these people. They were engaging in certain practices which were an extension of their wrong religious beliefs and traditions.

Enos describes Lamanites "feeding upon beasts of prey[.]" This gives us an interesting basis for evaluating Lamanite cosmology. If this was "idolatrous," then we are reading something more than just consumption of unclean animals under the Mosaic law. The Law of Moses forbad eating beasts of prey, to be sure,[62] but this was not just uncleanness, it is the first example of their idolatry.

What does eating animals of prey tell us about religious idolatry? It suggest that the Lamanites ate the animals as a form of worship, or religious sacrament. It suggests these beasts of prey were sought out specifically as the desired sacrament for people who wanted to benefit spiritually by this habit. It seems likely the "spirit" of the aggressive animal was a talisman to the Lamanites in their quest to become the predators who would dominate their Nephite

---

[62]For example, Lev. 11: 3 states: "Whatsoever parteth the hoof, and is clovenfooted, and cheweth the cud, among the beasts, that shall ye eat." To chew a cud rules out predators. Similarly, the birds of prey listed in verses 13-19 of that same Chapter are unclean: "And these are they which ye shall have in abomination among the fowls; they shall not be eaten, they are an abomination: the eagle, and the ossifrage, and the ospray, And the vulture, and the kite after his kind; Every raven after his kind; And the owl, and the night hawk, and the cuckow, and the hawk after his kind, And the little owl, and the cormorant, and the great owl, And the swan, and the pelican, and the gier eagle, And the stork, the heron after her kind, and the lapwing, and the bat."

opponents.

To pursue this lifestyle, the idolatry had to have an affect on the way they lived: "dwelling in tents, and wandering about in the wilderness[.]" Pursuing beasts of prey required a mobile, hunting social existence. They could not settle down and build permanent structures. By adopting a nomadic lifestyle these Lamanites may have been preserving a tradition relating back to the time of their ancestor's sojourn in the Trans-Arabian Peninsula. This may have been their intentional attempt to live a more authentic past lifestyle. This kind of excessive peroccupation with their ancestor's tradition is a kind of idolatry.

Next we read, "with a short skin girdle about their loins and their heads shaven[.]" A short, skin girdle implies a tradition which hearkens back to the Garden of Eden. When Adam and Eve found themselves naked, after their transgression, they put on an apron to cover their nakedness.[63] The girdle about their loins was likely related to this ancient tradition, once again as a way of asserting that they, the Lamanites, were the real thing. They followed the oldest tradition.

---

[63]See Gen. 3: 1-7: "Now the serpent was more subtil than any beast of the field which the Lord God had made. And he said unto the woman, Yea, hath God said, Ye shall not eat of every tree of the garden? And the woman said unto the serpent, We may eat of the fruit of the trees of the garden: But of the fruit of the tree which is in the midst of the garden, God hath said, Ye shall not eat of it, neither shall ye touch it, lest ye die. And the serpent said unto the woman, Ye shall not surely die: For God doth know that in the day ye eat thereof, then your eyes shall be opened, and ye shall be as gods, knowing good and evil. And when the woman saw that the tree was good for food, and that it was pleasant to the eyes, and a tree to be desired to make one wise, she took of the fruit thereof, and did eat, and gave also unto her husband with her; and he did eat. And the eyes of them both were opened, and they knew that they were naked; and they sewed fig leaves together, and made themselves aprons."

The girdle was made of "skin" and not leaves. This, too, had an ancient counterpart going back to the dawn of mankind.[64] Their idolatry reflected a lifestyle which was directly linked with a set of religious beliefs. Although there may have been actual counterparts in the true religion of the Nephites, the collective beliefs of the Lamanites were all corrupt.

The Lamanites' "skill was in the bow, and in the cimeter, and the ax." They were devoted to martial arts. They took comfort in their physical strength and martial prowess. However, we know from the battle between Goliath and David that there is no security in being adept with a sword and covered with armor.

Enos records "many of them did eat nothing save it was raw meat." This, too, may have been a link back to the original Lehi-Ishmael party's practice in the wilderness.[65] There was a time on the Arabian Peninsula when fires could not be lit because of danger posed by marauders. Eating raw meat may also have been a form of blood sacrifice or sacrament for these idolaters. We cannot be

---

[64]Gen. 3: 21: "Unto Adam also and to his wife did the Lord God make coats of skins, and clothed them."

[65]1 Ne. 17: 1-3: "And it came to pass that we did again take our journey in the wilderness; and we did travel nearly eastward from that time forth. And we did travel and wade through much affliction in the wilderness; and our women did bear children in the wilderness. And so great were the blessings of the Lord upon us, that while we did live upon raw meat in the wilderness, our women did give plenty of suck for their children, and were strong, yea, even like unto the men; and they began to bear their journeyings without murmurings. And thus we see that the commandments of God must be fulfilled. And if it so be that the children of men keep the commandments of God he doth nourish them, and strengthen them, and provide means whereby they can accomplish the thing which he has commanded them; wherefore, he did provide means for us while we did sojourn in the wilderness." The only two mentions of eating raw meat in the Book of Mormon are this one in 1 Nephi and Enos' account of the Lamanite practice.

certain, except that Enos links this practice to idolatry.

So what are the modern counterparts to these ancient practices? In addition to describing the ancient practices of an apostate people, Enos must have had a prophetic lesson in mind for us. What do we see today as a modern manifestation of these kinds of idolatrous practices? Are there those of us who seize upon traditions rather than upon the Gospel of Christ? Do some of us choose to follow a pattern laid down by traditions while ignoring requirements found in the Gospel? Do some of us practice strange dietary regimens as part of wrongly held religious beliefs? Are there those among us who believe martial arts are a higher form of religious pratice? Who can say Enos isn't speaking to us about our behavior in leaving this record. It would be a mistake to think he wrote only to preserve strange practices from the past without a concern for us as the future audience of his record. It would also be a mistake not to reconsider your own beliefs and practices to see if Enos was warning you.

Chapter 8

SOCIAL CONDITIONS

&nos next states:

> 21 And it came to pass that the people of Nephi did
> till the land, and raise all manner of grain, and of
> fruit, and flocks of herds, and flocks of all manner
> of cattle of every kind, and goats, and wild goats,
> and also many horses.

This brief disclosure tells us a great deal about the lifestyle of
these second- and third-generation Nephites. They farmed and
raised domesticated animals. Nephi's record tells us the original
emigrants brought seeds, but makes no specific mention of
importing animals. This is how Nephi described the departure from
the Arabian Peninsula: "And it came to pass that on the morrow,
after we had prepared *all things*, much fruits and meat from the
wilderness, and honey in abundance, and *provisions according to that
which the Lord had commanded us*, we did go down into the ship, with
all our loading and our seeds, and *whatsoever thing we had brought* with us,
every one according to his age; wherefore, we did all go down into
the ship, with our wives and our children." (1 Ne. 18: 6, emphasis
added.) The highlighted language may include domesticated animals.
In fact, the words: "provisions according to that which the Lord

had commanded us" could include anything. Second, "whatsoever thing we had brought with us" is equally broad and may have included some domestic animals. So we are left without knowing whether the collection of animals referred to by Enos were native to the new land or were transplants, descended from those which came with the Nephite ancestors from the old country.

There is also another possibility. The record of Nephi makes no attempt to provide details of the trans-oceanic voyage. The whole of it is contained in 1 Nephi, Chapter 18. We have nothing in the account to tell us whether or not there were stops along the way. It would seem likely there were, with periodic re-provisioning, even if they are never mentioned. Similarly, there is no mention of whether any animals were added as a result of hunting or trapping along the coastal route likely followed. We cannot rule out some of the domestic stock Enos mentions were handed-down from original stock arriving with the Nephites' first parents.

The reference to "horses" in this verse is the second time the word appears in the Book of Mormon. The earlier reference appears in 1 Ne. 18 and states: "And it came to pass that we did find upon the land of promise, as we journeyed in the wilderness, that there were beasts in the forests of every kind, … the ass and the horse, and the goat and the wild goat, and all manner of wild animals, which were for the use of men." The Book of Mormon has taken some criticism for including "horses" in the account. Critics assume the only horses which ever existed in the Americas were brought by European colonizers; a premise which is disproved by both the fossil record and pre-Columbian bones of horses.[66]

---

[66]Although a complete discussion of this is beyond the scope of this book, one recent reference to the discovery of horse bones in the Yucatan Peninsula appears in the October, 2003 *National Geographic Magazine*: "When dry, cenotes cracked and eroded, leaving soil packed

Because of the specific plants and animals noted in Enos' record, we conclude the agricultural practices of these Nephites made them stationary. They could only farm if they settled in a permanent location. This would result in Nephite city-building and a culture which allowed specialization. In contrast, the Lamanites appear to have been nomadic during Enos' time. These lifestyle differences appear in the first two generations and more or less endure for many generations. The differences between these two cultures both limited Lamanite mechanical and technological innovation and encouraged Nephite development. Consistent with these differences, Nephite innovation gave them an advantage until the end of the Book of Mormon record. Lamanite advances appear to follow and imitate the Nephite example. This historic legacy ensued as a result of the first generations' decision to be a city-building, agricultural people on the one hand (Nephites), and a nomadic people on the other hand (Lamanites).

Enos continues:

> 22 And there were exceedingly many prophets among us. And the people were a stiffnecked people, hard to understand.

It is significant that Enos felt no great jealousy at the presence of these "exceedingly many prophets" among the Nephites. They were welcome, expected and accepted. There was no centralized authority jealous of anyone's right to claim prophetic inspiration. Instead, at this point the Nephite people (Enos included) allowed for and accepted diverse prophetic callings. This is similar to Moses' tolerance and acceptance of others' right to receive revelation and

---

with the bones of small mammals, including a now extinct horse, a camelid, and a giant armadillo." (*Id.*, p. 93.)

to prophesy openly in the camp of Israel.[67] It is also akin to the Apostle Paul's and Philip the evangelist's visit to Caesarea, where they encounter both the prophet Agabus and four young prophetesses. These prophetic gifts were on display in the presence of the Apostle Paul without censure or jealousy. Rather, he accepted these as the proper right of these believing Saints.[68] Enos' record reminds us of how widely the Lord spreads gifts among His people. Today the gifts are spread beyond any central control. However, those who have gifts are oftentimes discouraged from making them known to others. This is particularly true of the prophetesses of our day. The only one we generally acknowledge is Eliza R. Snow.

---

[67] See Num. 11: 26-29: "But there remained two of the men in the camp, the name of the one was Eldad, and the name of the other Medad: and the spirit rested upon them; and they were of them that were written, but went not out unto the tabernacle: and they prophesied in the camp. And there ran a young man, and told Moses, and said, Eldad and Medad do prophesy in the camp. And Joshua the son of Nun, the servant of Moses, one of his young men, answered and said, My lord Moses, forbid them. And Moses said unto him, Enviest thou for my sake? would God that all the Lord's people were prophets, and that the Lord would put his spirit upon them!"

[68] See Acts 21: 8-14: "And the next day we that were of Paul's company departed, and came unto Caesarea: and we entered into the house of Philip the evangelist, which was one of the seven; and abode with him. And the same man had four daughters, virgins, which did prophesy. And as we tarried there many days, there came down from Judaea a certain prophet, named Agabus. And when he was come unto us, he took Paul's girdle, and bound his own hands and feet, and said, Thus saith the Holy Ghost, So shall the Jews at Jerusalem bind the man that owneth this girdle, and shall deliver him into the hands of the Gentiles. And when we heard these things, both we, and they of that place, besought him not to go up to Jerusalem. Then Paul answered, What mean ye to weep and to break mine heart? for I am ready not to be bound only, but also to die at Jerusalem for the name of the Lord Jesus. And when he would not be persuaded, we ceased, saying, The will of the Lord be done." Agabus' prophesy was fulfilled.

There have been and there are many others. Unlike Paul and Enos, we are oftentimes fearful and uncomfortable about gifted individuals and therefore discourage them. We are the poorer for it.

These "exceedingly many prophets" were working among a "stiffnecked people" who were "hard to understand," meaning, unwilling to comprehend. How wonderful this is to contemplate. Instead of stiffneckedness sending the Lord's gifts into immediate exile, it provokes an outpouring of prophecy to reclaim the wayward. These people do not immediately forfeit God's inspiration because of their unworthiness. He does not abandon them. He renews the call to them through an "exceedingly many prophets." What a wonderful and timely message in Enos.[69] God cares for His people. He works to reach out to them. In the end, it is only the persistent rejection of God which severs the link between God and His people.

The testimony of Jesus is the spirit of prophecy. (Rev. 19: 10.) We should encounter many prophets and prophetesses among any group of believers who claim to be Saints. When we do not, it is likely because our claims to sainthood have not been mirrored by living the life of a Saint.

Enos continues:

> 23 And there was nothing save it was exceeding harshness, preaching and prophesying of wars, and contentions, and destructions, and continually reminding them of death, and the duration of eternity, and the judgments and the power of God, and all these things--stirring them up continually to keep them in the fear of the Lord. I say there was

---

[69]Elder Boyd K. Packer spoke about the width and breadth of revelation coming in our own day in a talk given in the Semi-annual General Conference in October, 2005, titled *On Zion's Hill.* It is available on-line at www.lds.org.

> nothing short of these things, and exceedingly great
> plainness of speech, would keep them from going
> down speedily to destruction. And after this manner
> do I write concerning them.

The contrast between Enos' message about his own search for God and the message being preached among his contemporaries could not be more striking. He has been in a personal quest to find God, penetrate the veil and view things of all eternity. His people, however, are warned with harshness about the risks of destruction that hang over them. It is worth pausing to consider this contrast and what it implies for us.

Are men worthy to hear the higher things of eternity when they are stiffnecked and unwilling to comprehend? Enos' personal journey was motivated by the highest purposes. In contrast, this harsh warning to his peers sought only to preserve basic social order. The message is adapted to the needs of the audience. If the message from prophets is adapted to a disobedient and hardhearted people, then perhaps it is time to consider Enos' more positive example and message.

Enos juxtaposes the general wickedness of his time with his personal journey back to God's presence. The sinfulness of people around him did not affect his personal journey. He may have been the only one living at the time ready to penetrate the veil. We know nothing of the personal journeys of the "exceeding many prophets" who were crying for people to repent. Enos tells us nothing about them. But the societal failings which threatened to bring the Nephites to "speedy destruction" did not impair Enos' return to God. Of all the lessons left us by Enos, this is the most relevant. None of us is absolutely captive by our times. We are all free to receive **everything** God offers. It does not matter if your teachers, your friends, or your culture all fail to live up to the conditions which allow God to reveal Himself to them. Each one of us is still free to walk the path back to the presence of God, just as Enos did.

For the larger Nephite society the message was direct. It relied upon fear to motivate behavior. The prophets were "continually reminding them of death, and the duration of eternity, and the judgments and the power of God." This reliance upon fear of death and judgment by God may curtail gross misbehavior, but it never exalts. Contrast this with what motivated Enos. He contemplated "the words which [he] had often heard [his] father speak concerning eternal life, and the joy of the saints," which "sunk deep into [his] heart." (V. 3.) As he pondered on these positive and hopeful things, his "soul hungered." Order can often be imposed by using fear, but exaltation springs from love. What motivates you?

Enos writes next:

24 And I saw wars between the Nephites and Lamanites in the course of my days.

This description of the conflict at the early stages of Nephite/Lamanite struggle should not be confused with the kind of violence future generations would experience. These early "wars" were not deadly. It would not be until the next generation that actual killing began.[70] This is an early reference to internecine conflict at a point when the populations of both the Nephite and Lamanite peoples could not tolerate any significant loss of life without compromising their ability to continue as societies. These are second and third generation people who descended from

---

[70]The first mention of actual killing as a part of the Nephite/ Lamanite fighting is called "murder" by the record-keeper. We read in Jarom 1: 6: "they [meaning the Lamanites] loved murder." The early conflicts were called "war" but when death began it was called "murder."

numbers of perhaps as few as twenty or as many as sixty people to provide both sides with their population base. Even with intermarriage of the existing population,[71] and rapid reproduction rates, these two competitive societies could not afford to wage war to the point of killing one another. That would have to await a larger population base in future generations. For now, competition and conflict which is called "war" between these people likely drew blood, but stopped short of killing. When the sad day came that killing actually resulted from Nephite wars, the record calls it "murder" because a line has finally been crossed.

The picture Enos describes tells of competition between the Lamanite foragers and the Nephite farmers and ranchers. The likely cause of the conflict would arise from Lamanite envy of Nephite abundance. The Nephites were a stable, city building society who used specialized labor to produce crops, herds and flocks. The Lamanites were a nomadic society whose skill was in hunting and foraging for what they could find where they could find it. Perhaps it was more than envy. They may have had actual need as a result of over-hunting or seasonal availability of some food sources. The "warfare" apparently arose from Nephite efforts to repel the

---

[71]Enos' father Jacob condemned the Nephite practice of taking plural wives. This strongly suggests intermarriage with people who already lived in the Americas before the Lehite migration. See Jacob 1: 15. The availability of additional wives permitting this practice implies there was not only an imbalance between male and female population, but also that there were sufficient women of marriageable age to allow these relationships to be contracted at will. Without another source of women from a pre-existing population it is unlikely the Nephites could have produced such numbers in the ordinary course of only two generations. There are, of course, many hints in the Book of Mormon that an earlier Jaredite (to name only one) population already existed. For example, the Nephites used Jaredite names (several of Alma's sons bore Jaredite names) and Nephite coinage was Jaredite.

Lamanite raids. This makes sense. It is in the details of this record we find the authentic indications of an actual history. Joseph Smith did not invent this tale. He translated it from a record kept by an ancient, fallen people.

Chapter 9

ENOS IS BLESSED

$\mathcal{E}$nos closes his record with three interesting verses. The first states:

> 25 And it came to pass that I began to be old, and
> an hundred and seventy and nine years had passed
> away from the time that our father Lehi left
> Jerusalem.

As mentioned earlier, there may have been a significant amount of time between composing an account and ultimately etching it on the metal Plates of Nephi. Here Enos begins to reflect on his advancing age with the preface "and it came to pass." This preface is a signal that there has been some time between events. It can refer to any length of time. In this case it likely refers to many years. It also illustrates the likelihood that Enos, just as Nephi and Jacob, recorded events and then sometime later etched the events onto the Plates of Nephi. Nephi recorded his prophecies and history for many years before being commanded to make the plates upon which he, Jacob and Enos would then later etch. After the arrival in the new Promised Land Nephi wrote: "And it came to pass that the Lord commanded me, wherefore I did make plates of ore that I might engraven upon them the record of my people. And upon the plates which I made I did engraven the record of my father, and also our journeyings in the wilderness, and the prophecies of my father; and also many of mine own prophecies have I engraven upon them." (1 Ne 19: 1.) The "record of [Nephi's] father" and "mine own prophecies" were transcribed or engraven upon the newly made plates. They had been recorded much earlier than the fabrication of the plates themselves. It makes sense that all the authors who engraved on the plates would similarly wait until their mortal ministries were coming to an end, and then with a full view of their life's most important revelations begin to carve their permanent record.

We also learn 179 years have passed from the time Lehi left Jerusalem. Enos' father, Jacob, was born several years after the departure. Jacob died shortly before surrendering the Plates of Nephi to Enos. Enos wrote this account at the end of his life as he prepares to hand the plates on to his son, Jarom. The length of time suggests life-spans into the 80's or 90's for Nephi, Jacob and Enos.

He records next:

> 26 And I saw that I must soon go down to my grave, having been wrought upon by the power of God that I must preach and prophesy unto this people, and declare the word according to the truth which is in Christ. And I have declared it in all my days, and have rejoiced in it above that of the world.

This explanation of Enos' life is testimony he lived a prophet's life. He used his time in mortality to preach and prophesy to his contemporaries. However, this was not on his initiative. He was "wrought upon by the power of God" to minister. He had a message given to him. That is one of the measures of a true prophet. Such messengers feel the obligation imposed upon them from a higher source. They do not volunteer. They are drafted.

Enos' explanation is deeply personal. He was "called" to be the bearer of the plates but there is no indication in the record that he occupied a station similar to either Nephi or Jacob. Nephi was clearly the prophet-king of his people. (See 2 Ne. 5: 16-18; 6: 2.) Jacob was called and set apart as the presiding High Priest over the Nephites. (See 2 Ne. 6: 2; Jacob 2: 1-3.) Enos does not inform us that he held any official political or religious office. From his record, he seems to be nothing more than a layman who was given the responsibility of keeping the Plates of Nephi. Enos went to "wrestle" with the Lord apparently on his own initiative. Then having found God, he is entrusted with the obligation to preach and teach truth.

This account, like the later ministries of Abinadi and Samuel the Lamanite, involves a personal burden laid upon the messenger by the Lord. They, like Enos, were "wrought upon" by direct communication from the Lord. It serves to remind us that institutional sources of truth are not left unsupported by independent, inspired messengers. All teachers in The Church of Jesus Christ of Latter-day Saints are obligated to receive a personal commission to teach. Being "called" by a local leader is not enough. Without a commission from God it is forbidden for anyone to teach. "And the Spirit shall be given unto you by the prayer of faith; and if ye receive not the Spirit ye shall not teach." (D&C 42: 14.) It is a mandatory requirement in the Church for teachers to teach only by the Spirit. Without the Spirit, you are forbidden from teaching. Enos was "wrought upon" by the Spirit to teach and to prophesy. It might more properly be said: "if ye receive the Spirit ye cannot help but preach."

Enos leaves no information in his record about the

contemporary leaders of his day. Perhaps the same will be true of all contemporary leaders. It may be that those who are regarded as great while alive may not be remembered in a future day. Even their names may be forgotten, as Enos' record demonstrates. At the time of the New Testament, Cyrenius was a figure of such importance that Christ's birth was reckoned from the beginning of his appointment as governor of Syria. If it were not for Luke's brief mention in the second verse of Chapter 2 of his Gospel, however, his name would be forgotten to all but a few scholars delving into antiquity. It is not the importance of the position held by a man, nor the wealth he accumulates, nor the political power held, nor the religious position he attains during his life which makes a life memorable. It is the words of truth, the testimony of Christ, which persist and make a life significant. It is fidelity to Christ and teaching of Him which makes any of us significant.

The subject which occupied Enos was "the truth which is in Christ." Enos clearly understood who the Messenger of Truth was and who the source of all light for this world was. Modern revelation confirms: "For the word of the Lord is truth, and whatsoever is truth is light, and whatsoever is light is Spirit, even the Spirit of Jesus Christ." (D&C 84: 45.) We cannot find truth apart from Christ. Therefore, if you intend to preach of truth you are inevitably drawn to "the truth which is in Christ." All truth, as all light, originates from Christ.[72] These are some of the Gospel's

---

[72]See e.g., D&C 88: 6-14: "He that ascended up on high, as also he descended below all things, in that he comprehended all things, that he might be in all and through all things, the light of truth; Which truth shineth. This is the light of Christ. As also he is in the sun, and the light of the sun, and the power thereof by which it was made. As also he is in the moon, and is the light of the moon, and the power thereof by which it was made; As also the light of the stars, and the power thereof by which they were made; And the earth also, and the power thereof, even the earth

deepest concepts and Enos writes of this in plain simplicity. We continue to find the Book of Mormon to be "the most correct book" just as Joseph Smith declared it to be.

Enos preferred the message of the Gospel over the things of this world. This is also one of the signs of authentic messengers from God. There is always a trade-off between the things of this world and the things of God. God's messengers do not achieve worldly acclaim, public praise, financial gain or security in this life by publishing an authentic message from Christ. Such messages always insist the audience repent. The world has little use for a challenging message of repentance. Therefore, a choice is always required by Christ. You can never sit still if you are listening to Christ. His words will inevitably set you in motion, moving you away from the world and closer to Him. It will always ask for sacrifice, one of the foundational conditions of true worship. The price we pay for harmony with Christ demands we lay worldly success on the altar. Christ's true messengers rarely have more to sustain them than what is sufficient for their needs because the world does not reward His servants. Remember the wise men went to find Christ first at the king's residence and were disappointed. It required a further journey to find the lad living in a common house in Bethlehem,[73] in humble circumstances.

But note Enos' words about the trade-off he has made: He

---

upon which you stand. And the light which shineth, which giveth you light, is through him who enlighteneth your eyes, which is the same light that quickeneth your understandings; Which light proceedeth forth from the presence of God to fill the immensity of space--The light which is in all things, which giveth life to all things, which is the law by which all things are governed, even the power of God who sitteth upon his throne, who is in the bosom of eternity, who is in the midst of all things."

[73]Matt. 2: 9-11.

"rejoiced in it above that of the world." It has brought him joy, confidence in the presence of the Lord,[74] and deep satisfaction which nothing in this world can replace. The concluding verse of Enos' record tells us he possessed eternal life, or in other words, the greatest riches of all. "Seek not for riches but for wisdom, and behold, the mysteries of God shall be unfolded unto you, and then shall you be made rich. Behold, he that hath eternal life is rich." (D&C 6: 7.) Although eternal life may be of no economic value in the world, it nevertheless has the greatest value of all. Enos preferred the eternal view and was willing to give up what the world offers as a substitute.

Enos' final verse begins:

27 And I soon go to the place of my rest, which is with my Redeemer; for I know that in him I shall rest.

The word "rest" denotes exaltation, or receiving the fullness of God's glory. As modern revelation explains, "But they hardened their hearts and could not endure his presence; therefore, the Lord in his wrath, for his anger was kindled against them, swore that they should not enter into his rest while in the wilderness, *which rest is the fulness of his glory.*" (D&C 84: 24, emphasis added.) Enos confirms his calling and election are sure. He "knows" that he will enter into "rest" with his Redeemer. This is the crescendo of Enos' record. He

---

[74]See also D&C 121: 45, where we read: "Let thy bowels also be full of charity towards all men, and to the household of faith, and let virtue garnish thy thoughts unceasingly; then shall thy confidence wax strong in the presence of God; and the doctrine of the priesthood shall distil upon thy soul as the dews from heaven." Enos was able to be confident "in the presence of God" because of the trade-off he made. The trade is inevitable. As modern revelation describes it: "And verily I say unto thee that thou shalt lay aside the things of this world, and seek for the things of a better." (D&C 25: 10.)

was certain of exaltation. Enos has found the true religion. He believes and has lived in the same way as all those who have gained eternal life. Knowledge which makes any person's calling and election sure is obtained in the same way for every person. It is explained plainly in the *Lectures on Faith*, Sixth lecture in these words:

> 7. Let us here observe, that *a religion that does not require the sacrifice of all things never has power sufficient to produce the faith necessary unto life and salvation*; for, from the first existence of man, the faith necessary unto the enjoyment of life and *salvation never could be obtained without the sacrifice of all earthly things. It was through this sacrifice, and this only, that God has ordained that men should enjoy eternal life*; and it is through the medium of the sacrifice of all earthly things that men do actually know that they are doing the things that are well pleasing in the sight of God. *When a man has offered in sacrifice all that he has* for the truth's sake, not even withholding his life, and believing before God that he has been called to make this sacrifice because he seeks to do his will, *he does know, most assuredly, that God does and will accept his sacrifice and offering, and that he has not, nor will not seek his face in vain.* Under these circumstances, then, he can obtain the faith necessary for him to lay hold on eternal life.
> 8. *It is in vain for persons to fancy to themselves that they are heirs with those, or can be heirs with them, who have offered their all in sacrifice*, and by this means obtained faith in God and favor with him so as to obtain eternal life, *unless they, in like manner, offer unto him the same sacrifice, and through that offering obtain the knowledge* that they are accepted of him. (Emphasis added.)

These conditions are universal. Reputation, social standing, popularity and success must be burnt on the altar as a sacrifice before any person can learn they have eternal life. Since our lives are going to be lost anyway - and all the world has to offer will be meaningless - the trade is illusory. We are asked to give up what has never been ours to keep.

This life presents the opportunity to be heroic in the cause of Christ. But life is brief, the opportunity fleeting. Viewed in the proper light, the sacrifice of all things is nothing. You gain everything by giving up what is truly nothing. Only a fool would make the calculation otherwise.

He continues:

> And I rejoice in the day when my mortal shall put on immortality, and shall stand before him; then shall I see his face with pleasure,

The contrast between those who know they have eternal life and those who do not is stark. Enos knows seeing God will be pleasant for him. He has already seen Him. Because of this he has confidence in the next meeting with God. Compare that with the description of those who are unprepared for such a meeting: "Do ye suppose that ye shall dwell with him under a consciousness of your guilt? Do ye suppose that ye could be happy to dwell with that holy Being, when your souls are racked with a consciousness of guilt that ye have ever abused his laws? Behold, I say unto you that ye would be more miserable to dwell with a holy and just God, under a consciousness of your filthiness before him, than ye would to dwell with the damned souls in hell. For behold, when ye shall be brought to see your nakedness before God, and also the glory of God, and the holiness of Jesus Christ, it will kindle a flame of unquenchable fire upon you." (Mormon 9: 3-5.) This misery is the natural result of disappointment in choosing the world over eternal life. God does not need to punish. Men do that to themselves. "A man is his own tormenter and his own condemner. Hence the saying, They shall go into the lake that burns with fire and brimstone. The torment of disappointment in the mind of man is as exquisite as a lake burning with fire and brimstone. I say, so is the torment of man." (*TPJS*, p. 357.)

Enos tells us what he expects of the afterlife. He had the kind of hope which comes from a clear conscience before God. He had a secure expectation of exaltation because he gained it from God, who cannot lie. He was among those who "had departed the mortal life, firm in the hope of a glorious resurrection, through the grace of God the Father and his Only Begotten Son, Jesus Christ." (D&C 138: 14.)

His departing comment was the most significant of all:

> ...and he will say unto me: Come unto me, ye blessed, there is a place prepared for you in the mansions of my Father. Amen.

This reveals Enos' knowledge of another mystery of God. Remember earlier the dialogue between Enos and the Lord when he was told: "Enos, thy sins are forgiven thee, and thou shalt be blessed." The original punctuation of the Book of Mormon was provided by the print shop of E.B. Grandin as he typeset the first edition. Grandin's employee John H. Gilbert did the layout for the first printing. The punctuation and capitalizations in the Book of Mormon are not necessarily the only way to read the text. In this case, it might serve us well to consider another way to view these words. Consider the difference in meaning of the word "blessed" when read as a proper noun instead of an adjective: "Come unto me, ye Blessed. There is a place prepared for you in the mansions of my Father." If "Blessed" is another name given to Enos by the Lord, then here is another wonderful revelation about Enos' relationship with God.

When Enos went to wrestle with the Lord those many years earlier, the dialogue between them included the Lord's promise to Enos: "thou shalt be blessed." (Verse 5.) What if these words were punctuated: "thou shalt be Blessed." Meaning, the Lord gave to Enos the new name "Blessed" at the time of their first meeting. If so, then in the concluding verse of his record, Enos is telling us of the future time when the Lord will call him by the new name "Blessed" while assuring him of the mansion which belongs to him in the Father's kingdom.

One of the greatest responsibilities laid upon us in mortality is to gather titles, or names, while mortal. We learn from Isaiah that Christ had several name-titles which identify Him: "For unto us a child is born, unto us a son is given: and the government shall be upon his shoulder: and his name shall be called Wonderful, Counsellor, The mighty God, The everlasting Father, The Prince of Peace." (Isa. 9: 6.) In this passage Christ is clearly being given names. He would be known by other names, as well, including: "Redeemer" (1 Ne. 19: 18), "Lamb of God" (1 Ne. 10: 10), "Lion of Judah" (Rev. 5: 5), "Savior" (Mormon 7: 10), "Son of God" (Mark 1: 1), "Rabbi" (John 1: 49), "Son of Man" (D&C 61: 38), "Root of David" (Rev. 5: 5), "the Mighty One of Jacob" (1 Ne. 21: 26), "Master" (Matt. 26: 18), "Advocate" (D&C 110: 4), "Rock of Heaven" (Moses 7: 23), and many more. We are in mortality to similarly acquire titles by the things we do while here. One of the latter-day titles which men are obligated to obtain is "savior on Mount Zion" (Obad. 1: 21); a title which can only be earned by doing temple work for our kindred dead. We are to become "sons and daughters of God" (John 1: 12) by our obedience to Christ's Gospel. We are required to hold the name-title of "Redeemed" (Gal. 3: 13); for without the "Redeemed" there would be no

"Redeemer." We are "Beloved" (Col. 3: 12) if we are among the "Elect of God" (*Id.*). To have a part in His Kingdom we must be among the "Saints of God" (1 Ne. 14: 12). We must also become a "Member" of The Church of Jesus Christ of Latter-day Saints; an office held by all those who are baptized and confirmed into the Church (see D&C 20: 84). To be exalted we must also be one of those holding the title of "Member of the Church of the Firstborn" (D&C 76: 94). We must have a position assigned to us in "the general assembly" (D&C 107: 19). Many more names are associated with following the Lord's Gospel, including "Father" and "Mother," as well as "Sister" and "Brother." We must bear the titles "Husband" or "Wife" to have Eternal Life. (See D&C 132: 19-21.) We will not make an exhaustive list of the titles and names which must be acquired in mortality, but among those which are most desirable, certainly Enos' name-title "Blessed" would be included.

We know from Enos' concluding remarks that if we inherit a position alongside him in the afterlife we will be dwelling in a mansion in the kingdom of the Father. This brief little book by Enos is among the greatest of testimonies we have on record from any prophet in any generation.

Chapter 10

THE SEALING POWER:

Part I: Those Holding Authority

*L*earning principles or doctrines is of no value if they are not applied in individual lives. This book will fail in its purpose if you are not interested in obtaining the same result as Enos obtained. In the next three chapters we will discuss how Enos' blessings fit into the context of the sealing power.

The promise of eternal life that Enos received requires the authority referred to in scripture as 'the power to seal on earth and in heaven,' or the sealing power. This authority needs to be used on your behalf in order to obtain a promise of eternal life. Reading about others will never secure a thing for you. You must do it for yourself. As Joseph taught: "You, no doubt, will agree with us, and say, that *you have no right to claim the promises of the inhabitants before the flood; that you cannot found your hopes of salvation upon the obedience of the children of Israel* when journeying in the wilderness, *nor can you expect that the blessings which the apostles pronounced upon the churches of Christ eighteen hundred years ago, were intended for you.* Again, if others' blessings are not your blessings, others' curses are not your curses; you stand then in these last days, as all have stood before you, agents unto yourselves, to be judged according to your works." (*TPJS*, p. 12, emphasis added.) The first challenge is to learn who holds such power and how it can be used on your behalf. These remaining chapters will examine that question to encourage you to do as Enos.

The primary use of the sealing power is to perform ordinances for the salvation of mankind. It can and has been used for other purposes, but the primary benefit is in binding ordinances or covenants between God and man. In particular, the authoritative binding of families into marriages to endure past the grave.

With respect to the sealing power restored through Joseph Smith, the keys for that authority reside in only one man at one time. As the Lord stated in revelation: "I have appointed unto my servant Joseph to hold this power in the last days, and *there is never but one on the earth at a time on whom this power and the keys of this priesthood are conferred.*" (D&C 132: 7, emphasis added.) Therefore in The Church of Jesus Christ of Latter-day Saints only one person holds the keys to this authority. At this writing the one person is President Thomas S. Monson.

The full picture of this Gospel principle is much more nuanced and subtle than just a single statement. All the keys of this authority are conferred upon each person who is ordained to the Quorum of the Twelve Apostles. As President Gordon B. Hinckley explained: "The First Presidency and the Council of the Twelve Apostles, called and ordained to hold the keys of the priesthood, have the authority and responsibility to govern the Church, to administer its ordinances, to expound its doctrine, and to establish and maintain its practices. Each man who is ordained an Apostle and sustained a member of the Council of the Twelve is sustained as a prophet, seer, and revelator. ...Therefore, all incumbent members of the

Quorum of the First Presidency and of the Council of the Twelve have been the recipients of the keys, rights, and authority pertaining to the holy apostleship." (Hinckley, Gordon B. *God Is at the Helm*, Ensign CR, May, 1994, p. 53.) Although there is but one person authorized to exercise the keys in a fullness inside The Church of Jesus Christ of Latter-day Saints, the keys have been conferred upon more than one man; including all those in the First Presidency and Quorum of the Twelve.

Beyond these presiding authorities, however, the keys to seal marriages have also been passed along to men who seal marriages in every Temple. As President Joseph Fielding Smith explained: "I have said that only one man at a time on the earth holds the keys of this sealing power of the priesthood, but he may, and does, delegate power to others, and they officiate under his direction in the temples of the Lord. No man can officiate in these sealing ordinances until he receives the authority to do so by being set apart by the one who holds the keys, notwithstanding he may hold the priesthood. All the authority exercised in the temples is then, after all, the authority centered in one man. He has the power and calls upon others to officiate, and they seal upon us the keys and powers which, through our obedience, entitle us to become sons and daughters and members of the Church of the Firstborn, receiving all things in the kingdom. This is what we can get in the temple, so that we become members of the family, sons and daughters of God, not servants." (Smith, Joseph Fielding. *Doctrines of Salvation*. Edited by Bruce R. McConkie. 3 volumes. Salt Lake City: Bookcraft, 1956, vol. 2, p. 42.) The number of men who hold the sealing authority therefore includes those who serve as sealers in the temples of The Church of Jesus Christ of Latter-day Saints throughout the world. The number of sealers in the more than 100 working temples (at the time of this writing) would be in the thousands.

A second, undiscussed body of men have also been given sealing authority as a part of the ceremony often referred to as the "second anointing." As David John Buerger explains concerning this ordinance, the man, as part of the ceremony "is then anointed with oil on his head, after which he is ordained a king and a priest unto God to rule and reign in the House of Israel forever. ... He is also blessed with the following (as the officiator determines): the power to bind and loose, curse and bless, the blessings of Abraham, Isaac and Jacob; ..." (Buerger, David J. *The Mysteries of Godliness.* San Francisco: Smith Research Associates, 1994, p. 66.) President Boyd K. Packer taught: "The Prophet Joseph Smith said: 'The doctrine or sealing power of Elijah is as follows:—If you have power to seal on earth and in heaven, then we should be wise. The first thing you do, go and seal on earth your sons and daughters unto yourself, and yourself unto your fathers in eternal glory.' (*Teachings of the Prophet Joseph Smith.* Arranged by Joseph Fielding Smith. Salt Lake City: Deseret Book Company, 1972, p. 340.)" (Packer, Boyd K. *Covenants.* Ensign CR, May, 1987, p. 22, citation to *TPJS* in original.)

It should be clear to anyone who considers the matter that there are two distinct purposes involved in the sealing authority within these two categories of people holding the authority. With respect to the First Presidency and Quorum of the Twelve, the authority is given to them to regulate The Church of Jesus Christ of Latter-day Saints and to make their calling as presiding authorities over the Church possible. "The Melchizedek Priesthood holds the right of presidency, and has power and authority over all the offices in the church in all ages of the world, to administer in spiritual things. The Presidency of the High Priesthood, after the order of Melchizedek, have a right to officiate in all the offices in the church." (D&C 107:

8-9.) This authority to regulate the Church is the basis to call sealers for the various Temples, empowered with the authority to seal marriages. So the first category has sealing authority to regulate and preside in The Church of Jesus Christ of Latter-day Saints. With respect to the second category of those holding sealing authority, as a part of a second anointing, the purpose is limited to establishing the eternal family unit as a kingdom which will survive the grave. Their presiding authority is limited to their own family.

Those holding sealing power in the First Presidency and Quorum of the Twelve are required to attract a following and to preside in the Church. Those who have sealing power as a part of a second anointing are not permitted to establish a competing organization, attempt to attract followers, or claim the right to preside outside their own family. In this way the affairs of The Church of Jesus Christ of Latter-day Saints remains a "house of order."[75]

Many of the apostate polygamous sects claim authority which they say originated from President John Taylor. However, even if the original authority was granted by President Taylor, he made the delegation as the one holding the keys in the same manner in which Temple sealers are given sealing authority to act under the direction of the President. When President Taylor died, it would be up to President Wilford Woodruff to permit the keys to continue to be used. The idea that these keys could be passed down from sealer to sealer in an independent line of authority allowing a separate organization to be established in competition with The Church of Jesus Christ of Latter-day Saints is not only wrongheaded, it would run contrary to the scriptures. There is only one man authorized to

---

[75]D&C 132: 8: "Behold, mine house is a house of order, saith the Lord God, and not a house of confusion."

exercise the keys. (See D&C 132: 7, supra.)

There are others who hold sealing power independent of The Church of Jesus Christ of Latter-day Saints. John the Revelator tarries to minister to heirs of salvation and he holds these keys independent of the current earthly Church. As explained in modern revelation: " And *the Lord said unto me: John, my beloved, what desirest thou?* For if you shall ask what you will, it shall be granted unto you. And I said unto him: *Lord, give unto me power over death, that I may live and bring souls unto thee.* And the Lord said unto me: Verily, verily, I say unto thee, *because thou desirest this thou shalt tarry until I come in my glory*, and shalt prophesy before nations, kindreds, tongues and people. And for this cause the Lord said unto Peter: If I will that he tarry till I come, what is that to thee? For he desired of me that he might bring souls unto me, but thou desiredst that thou mightest speedily come unto me in my kingdom. I say unto thee, Peter, this was a good desire; but my beloved has desired that he might do more, or *a greater work yet among men* than what he has before done. Yea, he has undertaken a greater work; therefore I will make him as flaming fire and a ministering angel; *he shall minister for those who shall be heirs of salvation who dwell on the earth.*" (D&C 7: 1-6, emphasis added.) In modern revelation the Lord confirmed John remains to minister to men who dwell on the earth. As part of that ministry John has authority to minister using the sealing authority originally conferred upon him on the Mount of Transfiguration.[76] Therefore

---

[76]See e.g., Bruce R. McConkie, The Keys of the Kingdom, Ensign, May 1983, p. 21: "On a wondrous day in April of 1836, Moses and Elijah and Elias each come, bringing from their dispensations the keys and powers they had exercised as mortals. It is a day akin to that wondrous day 1800 years before on the Mount of Transfiguration. (See Matt. 17: 1-13.) Then it was, on the snowy mountain heights, after the Father had spoken from the cloud, that Moses and Elijah, both taken to heaven without tasting death, had come in their corporeal bodies to a

John is another person holding sealing authority independent of The Church of Jesus Christ of Latter-day Saints. He could use sealing authority as a part of his ministry. However, it would be improper to presume or expect John to establish a competing organization to the Church. We should expect his efforts to unite the Lord's people, not divide them. Anything otherwise would contradict the basic revelations organizing the work for the latter-days.

Just as John holds keys and continues to minister on assignment conferred from ordination in an earlier dispensation, the three Nephite Disciples hold the same sealing authority.[77] They also chose

---

temple not made with hands, and given for that day and time their keys and powers to Peter, James, and John."

[77]The extent of their authority is described briefly in 3 Ne. 28: 13-27: "And behold, the heavens were opened, and they were caught up into heaven, and saw and heard unspeakable things. And it was forbidden them that they should utter; neither was it given unto them power that they could utter the things which they saw and heard; And whether they were in the body or out of the body, they could not tell; for it did seem unto them like a transfiguration of them, that they were changed from this body of flesh into an immortal state, that they could behold the things of God. But it came to pass that they did again minister upon the face of the earth; nevertheless they did not minister of the things which they had heard and seen, because of the commandment which was given them in heaven. And now, whether they were mortal or immortal, from the day of their transfiguration, I know not; But this much I know, according to the record which hath been given--they did go forth upon the face of the land, and did minister unto all the people, uniting as many to the church as would believe in their preaching; baptizing them, and as many as were baptized did receive the Holy Ghost. And they were cast into prison by them who did not belong to the church. And the prisons could not hold them, for they were rent in twain. And they were cast down into the earth; but *they did smite the earth with the word of God*, insomuch that by his power they were delivered out of the depths of the earth; and therefore they could not dig pits sufficient to hold them. And thrice they were cast into a furnace and received no harm. And twice were they cast into a den of wild beasts; and behold they did play with the beasts as a child with a

to remain and minister to mortals.[78] These three also hold sealing authority independent of the Church. They continue to minister, and the Book of Mormon makes it clear though they will be among the latter-day Gentiles, the Gentiles will not know them.

In addition to these, there are others we do not know who also hold this authority. They are referred to as "[T]hose which I have reserved unto myself, holy men that ye know not of." (D&C 49: 8.) [Since we know of John and of the three Nephite Disciples, these other "holy men" must be in addition to these four.] This is no different from prior dispensations in which there were those who were not integrated into the Lord's main organized body of

---

suckling lamb, and received no harm. And it came to pass that thus they did go forth among all the people of Nephi, and did preach the gospel of Christ unto all people upon the face of the land; and they were converted unto the Lord, and were united unto the church of Christ, and thus the people of that generation were blessed, according to the word of Jesus. And now I, Mormon, make an end of speaking concerning these things for a time. Behold, I was about to write the names of those who were never to taste of death, but the Lord forbade; therefore I write them not, for they are hid from the world. But behold, I have seen them, and they have ministered unto me. And behold *they will be among the Gentiles, and the Gentiles shall know them not.*" (Emphasis added.)

[78]"And he said unto them: Behold, I know your thoughts, and *ye have desired the thing which John, my beloved, who was with me in my ministry, before that I was lifted up by the Jews, desired of me.* Therefore, more blessed are ye, for ye shall never taste of death; but ye shall live to behold all the doings of the Father unto the children of men, even until all things shall be fulfilled according to the will of the Father, when I shall come in my glory with the powers of heaven. And ye shall never endure the pains of death; but when I shall come in my glory ye shall be changed in the twinkling of an eye from mortality to immortality; and then shall ye be blessed in the kingdom of my Father. And again, ye shall not have pain while ye shall dwell in the flesh, neither sorrow save it be for the sins of the world; and all this will I do because of the thing which ye have desired of me, for *ye have desired that ye might bring the souls of men unto me, while the world shall stand.*" (3 Ne. 28: 6-9, emphasis added.)

believers.

God's chosen people were the descendants of Abraham, Isaac and Jacob/Israel. The sons of Jacob were the patriarchs of the twelve tribes of Israel. These were the Lord's people. The chosen people were in bondage in Egypt for generations until the time of Moses. Though raised in the household of Pharaoh, Moses killed an Egyptian and fled into the wilderness. There Moses encountered his future father-in-law, a Midianite. Jethro is referred to as the "priest of Midian." (See Exo. 3: 1; 18: 1.) This Midian priest was not among the children of Israel. He was living in the wilderness, apart from Israel and descended from Midian. However, it was from this non-Israelite man that Moses received ordination to the Melchizedek Priesthood. Moses' line of authority tracks back from Jethro to Esaias, a contemporary of Abraham.[79] Abraham was the father of both Isaac and Midian,[80] but Jethro's priesthood tracks back to a source independent of Abraham.

In addition, during the time when Israel was the chosen people, organized under a presiding hierarchy, with a Temple and formal priestly organization, there were men who held authority separate from the Israelite priestly order. They were independently functioning with Melchizedek Priesthood at a time when Israel was

---

[79]"And the sons of Moses, according to the Holy Priesthood which he received under the hand of his father-in-law, Jethro; And Jethro received it under the hand of Caleb; And Caleb received it under the hand of Elihu; And Elihu under the hand of Jeremy; And Jeremy under the hand of Gad; And Gad under the hand of Esaias; And Esaias received it under the hand of God. Esaias also lived in the days of Abraham, and was blessed of him." (D&C 84: 6-13.)

[80]We read in Genesis 25: 1-2: "Then again Abraham took a wife, and her name was Keturah. And she bare him Zimran, and Jokshan, and Medan, and *Midian* ..." (Emphasis added).

presided over by Aaronic or Levitical Priesthood. As to these separate Melchizedek Priesthood holders Joseph Smith taught: "All the prophets had the Melchizedek Priesthood and were ordained by God himself." (*TPJS*, p. 180.) As President Joseph Fielding Smith explained: "The keys of the Melchizedek Priesthood were held by ancient prophets and by Israel's prophets until the time of Moses. When the Lord took these keys away from Israel and left them the Aaronic Priesthood, there was still the necessity for the Lord to maintain prophets who held the Melchizedek Priesthood, but they were especially called and ordained in each instance by the direct edict from the Lord." (Smith, Joseph Fielding. *Answers to Gospel Questions, Volume 4. 5 Volumes.* Salt Lake City: Deseret Book, 1963, Vol. 4, p. 6.) A formal organization and priesthood order existed for God's chosen people throughout the Old Testament. However, alongside that formal order was another body of prophets who possessed a higher, Melchizedek Priesthood, authority. Therefore we know the Lord has not confined His work to a formal organization.

From this it is apparent there were and are those who hold sealing authority in addition to the presiding authorities of The Church of Jesus Christ of Latter-day Saints. The power to seal, which is essential for anyone to have their calling and election made sure (as Enos), is vested in our dispensation within these two sources: First, inside the Church this authority is held by the President of The Church of Jesus Christ of Latter-day Saints, members of the First Presidency of the Church, members of the Quorum of the Twelve Apostles, and by designated sealers who have had this authority conferred upon them by one of those holding the authority. In addition, those who have had their calling and election made sure through a Church ordinance have given to them the authority to seal their kingdom (i.e., inside their own family) as a part of the promises conferred upon them.

Second, ancillary to the Church the following persons have excercised sealing authority as a part of this dispensation as well: The Lord, from whom all keys originate, continues to have the right as the Second Comforter both to seal and confer sealing authority. John the Revelator and the three Nephite disciples have the authority and continue to minister. In addition, we have been told of unidentified "holy men ye know not of" who would also hold this authority. This undefined description of "holy men" cannot include John and the three Nephites because we know of them. So it must refer to yet others.[81] Also in this second category we know Elijah and Moses hold the authority, both of whom have appeared in this dispensation, whose assignments may allow them to return more often than we will ever know. Theirs are the keys which have been handed down from Joseph Smith and Oliver Cowdrey in a line of succession and are currently held by the First Presidency and Quorum of the Twelve. Finally, it would include those who have received sealing authority from any of these ancillary sources. It is possible all individuals who received sealing authority from these other sources are numbered among the "holy men [we] know not of" mentioned in D&C 49: 8, but we have no way of knowing that for certain. Nor do we have any way of knowing what number of unidentified holy people may be included in this category. One thing is clear, however, whenever the Lord has given authority to others while at the same time He has a chosen people organized as a Church or Kingdom, He does not permit these others to organize a body to compete with His chosen people. They support the effort

---

[81]They would likely include some from among those Twelve Disciples called from the "other sheep" visited by Christ after His appearance to the Nephites. (See 3 Ne. 16: 1-3.)

of the Lord. They do not break away and attract followers. The example of Lehi's people is not an exception to this rule because they never competed with the Jewish nation. The party led by Lehi left as an extended family to preserve themselves from destruction and had no further contact with the Jewish nation left behind. The various other examples of prophets holding sealing authority, from Adam, Enoch, Moses, Elijah, Elisha, Enos, Nephi, Moroni or Joseph Smith (to name only a few), did not organize a movement or order to compete with the Lord's chosen people, but always remained identified with them. Though they may have cried repentance to them, they did not establish a competing church, movement, or people. This truth ought to give sober pause to those who think independent authority handed down from President John Taylor justifies the various apostate movements in existence today. There is absolutely no Biblical or scriptural precedent for that.

Those who hold sealing authority from God will never be in conflict with or challenge the right of the President of the Church to exercise the keys of the sealing power as a part of the Church, and to regulate its use in all the world. Their authority will be exercised only inside their own family. Such men are meek and do not seek their own right to preside over others. Their "appointment" to the priesthood will be kept inside the bounds set by the Lord. These men support the House of the Lord, they do not divide it. We will discuss this further in the following chapters.

Chapter 11

THE SEALING POWER:

Part II: Receiving Authority Part of Calling and Elections

The term "calling and election" is describing an event in this life when a man is judged and given the promise of eternal life before the final Judgment Day. As Elder Bruce R. McConkie described it: "To have one's calling and election made sure is to be sealed up unto eternal life; it is to have the unconditional guarantee of exaltation in the highest heaven of the celestial world; it is to receive the assurance of godhood; *it is, in effect, to have the day of judgment advanced*, so that an inheritance of all the glory and honor of the Father's kingdom is assured prior to the day when the faithful actually enter into the divine presence to sit with Christ in his throne, even as he is 'set down' with his 'Father in his throne.' (Rev. 3: 21.)" (McConkie, Bruce R. *Doctrinal New Testament Commentary, Vol. 3,* p. 331, emphasis added.) Therefore, it is a personal (and private) announcement which occurs in mortality rather than the one the scriptures foretell on the final Day of Judgment. In Enos' case he knew while still in mortality he possessed the promise of eternal life. He gladly looked forward to the afterlife and being reunited with the Lord. You need to obtain that same promise and hold that same hope at being reunited with the Lord.

A person may have the sealing power conferred upon them without receiving their calling and election made sure. This was the case with Joseph Smith and Oliver Cowdrey who received the sealing power on April 3, 1836. (See D&C 110.) Joseph's calling and election was not until 1843.[82] (See D&C 132: 49: "For I am the Lord thy God, and will be with thee even unto the end of the world, and through all eternity; for verily *I seal upon you your exaltation*, and prepare a throne for you in the kingdom of my Father, with Abraham your father." Emphasis added.) Holding the authority does not automatically give the holder a guarantee of eternal life. They are two different things.

Those whose calling and election are made sure are given the promise of exaltation. They receive the promise of godhood in the afterlife. As Joseph taught: "Here, then, is eternal life-to know the only wise and true God; and *you have got to learn how to be Gods*

---

[82]It is likely Section 132 was received before 1843, or at least portions of it were received before then. A full discussion of that point is beyond the scope of this book. It is the author's view that Section 132 is comprised of between three and five different revelations received at different times, but on the same general subject matter. When Joseph dictated the revelation from memory at Hyrum's request Joseph included them all in the writing. Therefore Section 132 is an amalgamation of several different revelations received over many years. The only relevant point here is that the sealing power on the one hand was received at a different time than Joseph received his sure calling and election on the other hand. Further, there is no record of Oliver receiving his calling and election, although there is no question he received the sealing power with Joseph in the Kirtland Temple.

yourselves, and to be kings and priests to God, the same as all Gods have done before you, namely, by going from one small degree to another, and from a small capacity to a great one; from grace to grace, from exaltation to exaltation, until you attain to the resurrection of the dead, and are able to dwell in everlasting burnings, and to sit in glory, as do those who sit enthroned in everlasting power. And I want you to know that God, in the last days, while certain individuals are proclaiming his name, is not trifling with you or me." (*TPJS*, p. 346, emphasis added.) The promise of exaltation assures the recipient they will hold the power of God. The sealing power grants the recipient the opportunity to exercise a portion of God's power while still mortal.

In the Joseph Smith Translation of the Old Testament, there is a description of Melchizedek holding this power, and what it involved:

> Now Melchizedek was a man of faith, who wrought righteousness; and when a child he feared God, and stopped the mouths of lions, and quenched the violence of fire. And thus, having been approved of God, he was ordained an high priest after the order of the covenant which God made with Enoch, It being after the order of the son of God; which order came, not by man, nor the will of man; neither by father nor mother; neither by beginning of days nor end of years; but of God; And it was delivered unto men by the calling of his own voice, according to his own will, unto as many as believed on his name. For God having sworn unto Enoch and unto his seed with an oath by himself; that *every one being ordained after this order and calling should have power, by faith, to break mountains, to divide the seas, to dry up waters, to turn them out of their course; To put at defiance the armies of nations, to divide the earth, to break every band, to stand in the presence of God; to do all things according to his will*, according to his command,

subdue principalities and powers; and this by the will of the Son of God which was from before the foundation of the world. And men having this faith, coming up unto this order of God, were translated and taken up into heaven. And now, *Melchizedek was a priest of this order*, therefore he obtained peace in Salem, and was called the Prince of peace. (JST Gen. 14: 26-33., emphasis added.)

This is a description of the full potential of the sealing power. It can be used not only to bind ordinances as a part of the Gospel, but it may also be used in defense of the Saints of God. It may be used to control the elements, to part seas (as in Moses' case; see Ex. 14: 21), to call down fire from Heaven (as Elijah did; see 1 Kings 18: 30-38), or to stop rain and cause a famine (as in the case of Nephi; see Hel. 11: 4-17). It may be used to control the actions of others and prevent them from interrupting a message from God (as in the case of Abinadi; see Mosiah 13: 3), or from laying hands on them (as in the case of Christ; see Luke 4: 29-30), or to hold hostile armies at bay (as in the case of Enoch; see Moses 7: 13). It will be used by two prophet messengers sent to Jerusalem in some future mission to preserve latter-day Israel from destruction through the days of their ministry (see Rev. 11: 1-7).

It is the sealing authority which must bind covenant blessings in order for them to endure into the next life. Without it nothing, including associations or expectations for the next life, are assured to anyone. "*All covenants, contracts, bonds, obligations, oaths, vows, performances, connections, associations, or expectations, that are not made and entered into and sealed by the Holy Spirit of promise*, of him who is anointed, both as well for time and for all eternity, and that too most holy, by revelation and commandment through the medium of mine anointed, whom I have appointed on the earth to hold this power (and I have appointed unto my servant Joseph to hold this power in the last days, and there is never but one on the earth at a time on whom this power and the keys of this priesthood are conferred), *are of no efficacy, virtue, or force in and after the resurrection* from the dead; for all contracts that are not made unto this end have an end when men are dead." (D&C 132: 7, emphasis added.) These words are deliberately broad. They cover everything from covenants and oaths to associations and connections. Everything we hope to have in the afterlife can only be ours if they are promised through the sealing power. This is why the sealing power is always involved in making a person's calling and election sure. Nothing can be "sure" without it being sealed by a promise from God.

Joseph Smith said a great deal about this important subject. Speaking of Latter-day Saints' obligation to become saviors on Mount Zion he taught: "But how are they to become saviors on Mount Zion? By building their temples, erecting their baptismal fonts, and going forth *and receiving all the* ordinances, baptisms, confirmations, washings, anointings, *ordinations and sealing powers upon their heads*, in behalf of all their progenitors who are dead, and redeem them *that they may come forth in the first resurrection and be exalted to thrones of glory* with them; and herein is the chain that binds the hearts of the fathers to the children, and the children to the fathers, which fulfills the mission of Elijah. And I would to God that this temple was now done, that we might go into it, and go to work and improve our time, and *make use of the seals while they are on earth*." (*TPJS*, p. 330, emphasis added.) The time for this to happen is while you are still on earth, still mortal. You need to receive "ordinations and sealing powers upon [your] head" if you hope to "be exalted to thrones of glory." This is the only way in which these expectations can be guaranteed for the afterlife.

Joseph tied the sealing authority to having your calling and election made sure: "Peter exhorts us to make our calling and election sure. This is the sealing power spoken of by Paul in other places." (*TPJS*, p. 149.) The reference to Peter is found in 2 Peter 1: 8-11.[83] The reference to Paul is found in 2 Cor. 1: 22: "Who hath also *sealed us*, and given the earnest of the Spirit in our hearts." Eph. 1: 13: "In whom ye also trusted, after that ye heard the word of truth, the gospel of your salvation: in whom also after that ye believed, *ye were sealed with that holy Spirit of promise*," and Eph. 4: 30: "And grieve not the holy Spirit of God, whereby *ye are sealed unto the day of redemption*." (Emphasis added in all quotes.)

Joseph Smith also taught: "This principle ought (in its proper place) to be taught, for God hath not revealed anything to Joseph, but what He will make known unto the Twelve, and even the least Saint may know all things as fast as he is able to bear them, for the day must come when no man need say to his neighbor, Know ye the Lord; for all shall know Him (who remain) from the least to the greatest. How is this to be done? *It is to be done by this sealing power, and the other Comforter spoken of, which will be manifest by revelation*." (*TPJS*, p. 149, emphasis added.) Here Joseph ties the Second Comforter to the sealing power. He also does this at *TPJS*, p. 150. Although they are two distinct things, one being the person of Jesus Christ, the other being a covenantal promise of exaltation, they are related. The fact they are not synonyms is shown in Joseph's life. He received

---

[83]"For if these things be in you, and abound, they make you that ye shall neither be barren nor unfruitful in the knowledge of our Lord Jesus Christ. But he that lacketh these things is blind, and cannot see afar off, and hath forgotten that he was purged from his old sins. Wherefore the rather, brethren, *give diligence to make your calling and election sure: for if ye do these things, ye shall never fall: For so an entrance shall be ministered unto you abundantly into the everlasting kingdom of our Lord and Saviour Jesus Christ*." (Emphasis added.)

visits from Christ in the Sacred Grove in 1820 (JS-H 1: 17), in Hiram, Ohio with Sidney Rigdon in 1832 (D&C 76: 20-24), and again in the Kirtland Temple in 1836 (D&C 110: 1-10). But Joseph's calling and election was not recorded, as we have already seen, until 1843 (D&C 132: 49). That section likely included up to five separate revelations, and we will assume for our purposes that the calling and election occurred at or near the date recorded.

When Joseph's exaltation was sealed upon him he also had the sealing authority reconfirmed. Just as Joseph's promise of exaltation is made we read also in D&C 132: 46-49: "And verily, verily, I say unto you, that *whatsoever you seal on earth shall be sealed in heaven*; and whatsoever you bind on earth, in my name and by my word, saith the Lord, it shall be eternally bound in the heavens; and whosesoever sins you remit on earth shall be remitted eternally in the heavens; and whosesoever sins you retain on earth shall be retained in heaven. And again, verily I say, whomsoever you bless I will bless, and whomsoever you curse I will curse, saith the Lord; for I, the Lord, am thy God. And again, verily I say unto you, my servant Joseph, that whatsoever you give on earth, and to whomsoever you give any one on earth, by my word and according to my law, it shall be visited with blessings and not cursings, and with my power, saith the Lord, and shall be without condemnation on earth and in heaven. For I am the Lord thy God, and will be with thee even unto the end of the world, and through all eternity; for verily *I seal upon you your exaltation*, and prepare a throne for you in the kingdom of my Father, with Abraham your father." (Emphasis added.) This promise was recorded in 1843. Joseph had already received the sealing authority from Elijah in 1836. However, once his calling and election was made sure, in the context of establishing his own kingdom (family), the Lord reiterates the sealing authority upon Joseph.

Joseph also referred to the sealing authority in connection with the Second Coming of Christ: "Four destroying angels holding power over the four quarters of the earth until the servants of God are sealed in their foreheads, which signifies sealing the blessing upon their heads, meaning the everlasting covenant, *thereby making their calling and election sure*. When a seal is put upon the father and mother, it secures their posterity, so that they cannot be lost, but will be saved by virtue of the covenant of their father and mother." (*TPJS*, p. 321, emphasis added.) Here Joseph also refers to the binding effect which the covenant has upon children belonging to parents holding sealing authority. Part of the covenant secures to them every promise made to them, including the right to claim their posterity in the afterlife. Hence the comment about the children "cannot be lost" to those parents who have these promises extended to them.

In the context of family, exaltation and the sealing power, Joseph taught: "Again: The doctrine or sealing power of Elijah is as follows:-*If you have power to seal on earth and in heaven*, then we should be wise. *The first thing you do, go and seal on earth your sons and daughters unto yourself*, and yourself unto your fathers in eternal glory, and go ahead, and not go back, but use a little wisdom, and *seal all you can*, and *when you get to heaven tell your Father that what you seal on earth should be sealed in heaven, according to his promise*. I will walk through the gate of heaven and claim what I seal, and those that follow me and my counsel." (*TPJS*, p. 340, emphasis added.) Joseph understood when the authority is given to any couple whose calling and election is sure, they were expected to use it to secure for themselves their kingdom. In this sense there is no reason for individuals holding this authority to reach outside the family, to attract attention, seek for a following or try to command others. It is enough of a work to secure the exaltation for yourself and your family should such authority be conferred upon you.

Commenting upon this same right and obligation Joseph said, " The greatest responsibility in this world that God has laid upon us is to seek after our dead. The Apostle says, 'They without us cannot be made perfect;' (Hebrews 11:40) for *it is necessary that the sealing power should be in our hands to seal our children and our dead for the fulness* of the dispensation of times-a dispensation to meet the promises made by Jesus Christ before the foundation of the world for the salvation of man." (*TPJS*, p. 356.)

So we see the sealing power and having one's calling and election made sure are connected with each other. Joseph taught they were tied together, as well as receiving the Second Comforter. Joseph understood the fullness of the Gospel of Jesus Christ tied together the heavens and the earth. It tied together generations; life and afterlife.

Although these things are most sacred and require a good deal of light for a person to be able to keep them in proper perspective, Joseph spoke openly about them. President Marion G. Romney also spoke openly about them in the April, 1977 General Conference. President Romney tied the doctrine to Enos' experience. He taught:

> Now, concerning the third phase of our theme, "the more sure word of prophecy" (D&C 131:5), which is obtained by making one's "calling and election sure" (2 Pet. 1:10), the Prophet Joseph said: "After a person has faith in Christ, repents of his sins, and is baptized for the remission of his sins and receives the Holy Ghost, (by the laying on of hands) ... then let him continue to humble himself before God, hungering and thirsting after righteousness, and

living by every word of God, and *the Lord will soon say unto him, Son, thou shalt be exalted.* When the Lord has thoroughly proved him, and finds that the man is determined to serve Him at all hazards, then the man will find his calling and his election made sure, then it will be his privilege to receive the other Comforter, which the Lord hath promised the Saints, as is recorded in the testimony of St. John." (Teachings of the Prophet Joseph Smith, p. 150.)

In the eighty-eighth section of the Doctrine and Covenants is recorded a revelation in which the Lord, addressing some of the early Saints in Ohio, said: "I now send upon you another Comforter, even upon you my friends, that it may abide in your hearts, even the Holy Spirit of promise; which other Comforter is the same that I promised unto my disciples, as is recorded in the testimoony of John. 'This Comforter is the promise which I give unto you of eternal life, even glory in the celestial kingdom' (D&C 88: 3-4.) *I should think that all faithful Latter-day Saints would want that more sure word of prophecy, that they were sealed in the heavens and had the promise of eternal life in the kingdom of God.*" (History of the Church of Jesus Christ of Latter-day Saints, 5: 388.)

As I read the sacred records, I find recorded experiences of men in all dispensations who have had this more sure anchor to their souls, this peace in their hearts. Lehi's grandson Enos so hungered after righteousness that he cried unto the Lord until "there came a voice unto [him], saying: Enos, they sins are forgiven thee, and thou shalt be blessed." (Enos 1: 5.) Years later Enos revealed the nature of this promised blessing when he wrote: "I soon go to the place of my rest, which is with my Redeemer; for I know that in him I shall rest. And I rejoice in that day when my mortal shall put on immortality, and shall stand before him; then shall I see his face with pleasure, and *he will say unto me: Come unto me, ye blessed, there is a place prepared for you in the mansions of my Father.*" (Enos 1: 27.) (Romney, Marion G., *The light of Christ*. Ensign, CR, May, 1977, p. 43, emphasis added.)

In the October 1977 Semi-annual General Conference, Elder Bruce R. McConkie also spoke about this subject. He taught:

> Blessing nine: We have power to make our calling and election sure, so that while we yet dwell in mortality, having overcome the world and been true and faithful in all things, we shall be sealed up unto eternal life and have the unconditional promise of eternal life in the presence of Him whose we are. Our revelations say: "The more sure word of prophecy means a man's knowing that he is sealed up unto eternal life, by revelation and the spirit of prophecy, through the power of the Holy Priesthood." (D&C 131: 5.) During the latter years of his ministry, in particular, the Prophet Joseph Smith pleaded fervently with the Saints to press forward in righteousness until they made their calling and election sure, until they heard the heavenly voice proclaim: "Son, thou shalt be exalted." (Teachings of the Prophet Joseph Smith, p. 150.) He himself became the pattern for all such attainment in this dispensation, when the voice from heaven said to him: "I am the Lord thy God, and will be with thee even unto the end of the world, and through all eternity; for verily I seal upon you your exaltation, and prepare a throne for you in the kingdom of my Father, with Abraham your father." (D&C 132: 49.)
>
> Blessing ten: We have the power—and it is our privilege—so to live, that becoming pure in heart, we shall see the face of God while we yet dwell as mortals in a world of sin and sorrow. This is the crowning blessing of mortality. It is offered by that

God who is no respecter of persons to all the faithful in his kingdom.

"Verily, thus saith the Lord: It shall come to pass that every soul who forsaketh his sins and cometh unto me, and calleth on my name, and obeyeth my voice, and keepeth my commandments, shall see my face and know that I am." (D&C 93: 1.) "And again, verily I say unto you that it is your privilege, and a promise I give unto you that have been ordained unto this ministry"—he is speaking now to those who hold the Melchizedek Priesthood—"that inasmuch as you strip yourselves from jealousies and fears, and humble yourselves before me, for ye are not sufficiently humble, the veil shall be rent and you shall see me and know that I am—not with the carnal neither natural mind, but with the spiritual. "For no man has seen God at any time in the flesh, except quickened by the Spirit of God. Neither can any natural man abide the presence of God, neither after the carnal mind. Ye are not able to abide the presence of God now, neither the ministering of angels; wherefore, continue in patience until ye are perfected." (D&C 67: 10-13.)

These, then, are the ten blessings of the priesthood, the Holy Priesthood, after the order of the Son of God, the priesthood which the saints in ancient days called after Melchizedek to avoid the too frequent repetition of the name of Diety. (Elder Bruce R. McConkie, the *Ten Blessings of the Priesthood*, Ensign, CR, November 1977, p, 33, emphasis added.)

Today we hear less often about this subject. Even so, it remains as always a central part of the Restored Gospel of Jesus Christ and an important reason for Joseph Smith's mission. Even if it now requires some effort to search these teachings out because we fail to commonly teach about this subject, it is still our responsibility to do so. Joseph cleaned his garments of our blood by leaving these teachings for us. We may not remove the stain from our own garments unless we learn at last to heed his warning.

Chapter 12

THE SEALING POWER:

Part III: The Kind of Person Who Receives

It would be impossible to understand the kind of man Enos was without understanding the kind of men who are entrusted with sealing power. Remember Enos had a promise of eternal life, he obtained a covenant for the latter-day restoration of the Lamanites, and he was called by the Lord "Blessed." To understand how he experienced this we need to understand the character of all those who have such experiences. It is not so much what they *did* as what they *are*. Fortunately, the Book of Mormon gives us a wealth of information from which to understand this part of the Gospel and to know what kind of person each of us is expected to become.

The most detailed explanation of the criteria for someone receiving the sealing power is found in Helaman, Chapters 10 and 11. Before using other sources, we will examine that account carefully. It is set out at length below because it is so important a resource on this topic. It states:

Behold, thou art Nephi, and I am God. Behold, I

declare it unto thee in the presence of mine angels, that *ye shall have power over this people*, and shall smite the earth with famine, and with pestilence, and destruction, according to the wickedness of this people. Behold, *I give unto you power, that whatsoever ye shall seal on earth shall be sealed in heaven; and whatsoever ye shall loose on earth shall be loosed in heaven*; and thus shall ye have power among this people. And thus, *if ye shall say* unto this temple it shall be rent in twain, *it shall be done.* And *if ye shall say* unto this mountain, Be thou cast down and become smooth, *it shall be done.* And behold, *if ye shall say* that God shall smite this people, *it shall come to pass.* (Hel. 10: 6-10.)

Nephi is given authority to speak the will of God. God will ratify whatever Nephi commits the Lord to do. If you take these words literally, Nephi is essentially being given the power of God even though he is a mere mortal. He became a "god among us" by this pronouncement.[84] This teaching is the very reason Christ was persecuted and killed. Christ asserted the right to bear these names, to hold these titles. He was a "God among us," the true Emmanuel. But Christ is not jealous of His position as a Son of God. He came to make others sons of God. "But as many as received him, to them gave he power to become the sons of God." (John 1: 12.) The full meaning of becoming such a son of God while yet mortal, however, is not often understood. The breadth of what being a son of God implies caused Paul to write: "For this cause I bow my knees unto the Father of *our Lord Jesus Christ, Of whom the whole family in heaven and earth is named*, That he would grant you, according to *the riches of*

---

[84]The phrase "god among us" is taken from the name Immanuel; which was one of the names associated with Christ. See Isa. 7: 14. The obligation to take upon you the name of the Son found in the sacrament prayer (D&C 20: 77) is linked to the role or title you acquire in mortality. This was discussed earlier in Chapter 9.

his glory, to be strengthened with might by his Spirit in the inner man; That Christ may dwell in your hearts by faith; that ye, being rooted and grounded in love, May be able to comprehend with all saints what is the breadth, and length, and depth, and height; And to know *the love of Christ, which passeth knowledge*, that ye might be filled with all the fulness of God." (Eph. 3: 14-19, emphasis added.) Paul received this same fullness from Christ; Paul had this same experience of being one of the sons of God. Paul's phrase "the riches of his glory" is altogether appropriate.

So let us assume the words recorded in Helaman spoken to Nephi can be taken literally; how did Nephi use this power from God? He used it in meekness. Meekness means a person voluntarily restrains themselves to exercise the absolute minimum control or authority over others. He never did or said anything on his own initiative which would obligate God to act. Instead he asked God to do things, always leaving it to the Lord to either grant or deny the request. In fact Nephi's meekness required the Lord to command him before he spoke a threat to his rebellious peers. We read:

> And now behold, *I command you, that ye shall go and declare unto this people, that thus saith the Lord God, who is the Almighty: Except ye repent ye shall be smitten*, even unto destruction. And behold, now it came to pass that when the Lord had spoken these words unto Nephi, he did stop and did not go unto his own house, but did return unto the multitudes who were scattered about upon the face of the land, and began to declare unto them the word of the Lord which had been spoken unto him, concerning their destruction if they did not repent. Now behold, notwithstanding that great miracle which Nephi had done in telling them concerning the death of the chief judge, they did harden their hearts and did not hearken unto the words of the Lord. *Therefore Nephi did declare unto them the word of the Lord, saying: Except*

ye repent, thus saith the Lord, ye shall be smitten even
unto destruction. (Hel 10: 11-14.)

What sort of man is it who will only deliver a threatening
message of destruction when he is commanded to do so by God?
The answer is a meek man; a man who values the lives of his
fellowman and would not deliberately harm another. We have
considered meekness in Chapter 7. It is a rare virtue. Men rarely
show the kind of restraint Nephi showed. Throughout history men
have used control, or compulsion, or dominion to gratify their
pride and satisfy their vain ambition as a sign of magnifying their
power, holding office, or discharging callings.[85] The warning given

---

[85]"That the rights of the priesthood are inseparably connected
with the powers of heaven, and that the powers of heaven cannot be
controlled nor handled only upon the principles of righteousness. That
they may be conferred upon us, it is true; but when we undertake to
cover our sins, or to gratify our pride, our vain ambition, or to exercise
control or dominion or compulsion upon the souls of the children of
men, in any degree of unrighteousness, behold, the heavens withdraw
themselves; the Spirit of the Lord is grieved; and when it is withdrawn,
Amen to the priesthood or the authority of that man. Behold, ere he is
aware, he is left unto himself, to kick against the pricks, to persecute the
saints, and to fight against God. We have learned by sad experience that
it is the nature and disposition of almost all men, as soon as they get a
little authority, as they suppose, they will immediately begin to exercise
unrighteous dominion. Hence many are called, but few are chosen. No
power or influence can or ought to be maintained by virtue of the
priesthood, only by persuasion, by long-suffering, by gentleness and
meekness, and by love unfeigned; By kindness, and pure knowledge,
which shall greatly enlarge the soul without hypocrisy, and without
guile." (D&C 121: 36-42.) It is interesting this caution warns of
"persecuting the saints" and "fighting against God" without **mentioning
the Church itself**. Therefore it is possible for Church members or
leaders to "persecute the saints" and "fight against God" whenever we
attempt to use coercion against another. This cautionary warning should
make anyone pause before they decide they have the right to demand,
intimidate, manipulate, control or exercise dominion over another
person. That, of course, is an eye-opening thought to contemplate. It

us in Section 121 came because "[w]e have learned by sad experience that it is the nature and disposition of almost all men, as soon as they get a little authority, as they suppose, they will immediately begin to exercise unrighteous dominion." (Verse 39.)

It is difficult for us to see the right pattern, the Christ-like pattern, contained in the Book of Mormon because our modern social systems depend on control, dominion and compulsion for success. Between boycotts, picketing, public ridicule, social ostracism, political correctness and peer pressure, our day has little need to rely upon meekness, kindness, gentleness, love unfeigned and pure knowledge to convince another to change their lives. The methods used by the sons of God are considered weak when compared to modern management techniques. In the end, however, it is *only* the tools of the meek which actually produces change in the hearts of men. If compulsion is used, as soon as compulsion is removed the modern management techniques fail. None of it will survive the grave. Those who delude themselves into thinking they have "magnified their calling" by using such tools to increase statistical performance in their ward, or stake or mission will likely never understand the meekness of our Lord. They will fail in their attempt to become one of the sons of God. They will never be trusted with the power of God. They cannot be trusted to hold the power which would make them another Emmanuel.

The account continues:

> And it came to pass that thus *he did go forth in the Spirit*, from multitude to multitude, *declaring the word*

---

reminds us we must be careful about who we think we can force to bend to our will. Generally we have no right to attempt to force anyone to do anything; only the obligation to persuade using kindness, love and pure knowledge.

of God, even until he had declared it unto them all, or sent it forth among all the people. And it came to pass that *they would not hearken unto his words*; and there began to be contentions, insomuch that they were divided against themselves and began to slay one another with the sword. And thus ended the seventy and first year of the reign of the judges over the people of Nephi. And now it came to pass in the seventy and second year of the reign of the judges that the contentions did increase, insomuch that there were wars throughout all the land among all the people of Nephi. And it was this secret band of robbers who did carry on this work of destruction and wickedness. And this war did last all that year; and in the seventy and third year it did also last. And it came to pass that in this year *Nephi did cry unto the Lord*, saying: O Lord, do not suffer that this people shall be destroyed by the sword; but O Lord, rather let there be a famine in the land, to stir them up in remembrance of the Lord their God, and *perhaps they will repent and turn unto thee*. (Hel. 10: 17-11: 4.)

Nephi asked, but did not demand. He made the request of the Lord out of his hope that famine may humble the same people who rejected him. In response to being personally rejected Nephi did nothing. The power he had been given was never used to vindicate himself or his message. But when the people began to kill each other, then Nephi sought to preserve the people who rejected his message. Nephi explained to the Lord his hope that perhaps a famine may cause the people to repent, stop killing each other, and return to follow God. Nephi did not attempt to gain any favor for himself with the power he had been granted, but he did not want to see these people kill one another. Nephi is both meek and charitable. They may abuse him, but he did nothing but return kindness.

This is the kind of man to whom the Lord entrusts the sealing power. This is the kind of man who can be another Emmanuel. This is the kind of man Christ was. There are few meek men. But it is only the meek who can be given this authority by the Lord.

It is important to understand this doctrine because it is the key to understanding what the fullness of Christ's Gospel involves. You need to understand this in order to see the path which lies strait[86] before you. You need to become meek in order to be one of the sons of God. The first step is to see clearly these teachings contained in the Book of Mormon. Unless you see them you cannot hope to understand what you must correct in your life. Always keep in mind God is no respecter of persons, and He gives liberally to all those who search with a sincere heart, having pure intent. For anyone who is meek and can be trusted, if they seek these things God will give them.

The record continues:

> And so it was done, according to the words of Nephi. And there was a great famine upon the land, among all the people of Nephi. And thus in the seventy and fourth year the famine did continue, and the work of destruction did cease by the sword but became sore by famine. And this work of destruction did also continue in the seventy and fifth year. For the earth was smitten that it was dry, and did not yield forth grain in the season of grain; and the whole earth was smitten, even among the Lamanites as well as among the Nephites, so that they were smitten that they did perish by thousands in the more wicked parts of the land. And it came to pass

---

[86]This is the right spelling. The correct word is "strait" and not "straight."

that the people saw that they were about to
perish by famine, and they began to remember
the Lord their God; and they began to remember
the words of Nephi. And the people began to
plead with their chief judges and their leaders,
that they would say unto Nephi: Behold, we
know that thou art a man of God, and therefore
cry unto the Lord our God that he turn away
from us this famine, lest all the words which
thou hast spoken concerning our destruction be
fulfilled. And it came to pass that the judges did
say unto Nephi, according to the words which
had been desired. And it came to pass that when
Nephi saw that the people had repented and did
humble themselves in sackcloth, he cried again
unto the Lord, saying: O Lord, behold this
people repenteth; and they have swept away the
band of Gadianton from amongst them
insomuch that they have become extinct, and
they have concealed their secret plans in the
earth. Now, O Lord, because of this their
humility *wilt thou* turn away thine anger, and let
thine anger be appeased in the destruction of
those wicked men whom thou hast already
destroyed. *O Lord, wilt thou* turn away thine anger,
yea, thy fierce anger, and cause that this famine
may cease in this land. *O Lord, wilt thou hearken
unto me*, and cause that it may be done according
to my words, and send forth rain upon the face
of the earth, that she may bring forth her fruit,
and her grain in the season of grain. O Lord,
thou didst hearken unto my words when I said,
Let there be a famine, that the pestilence of the
sword might cease; and I know that thou wilt,
even at this time, hearken unto my words, for
thou saidst that: If this people repent I will spare
them. Yea, O Lord, and thou seest that they
have repented, because of the famine and the
pestilence and destruction which has come unto

them. And now, *O Lord, wilt thou* turn away thine anger, and try again if they will serve thee? And if so, O Lord, thou canst bless them according to thy words which thou hast said. And it came to pass that in the seventy and sixth year the Lord did turn away his anger from the people, and caused that rain should fall upon the earth, insomuch that it did bring forth her fruit in the season of her fruit. And it came to pass that it did bring forth her grain in the season of her grain. (Hel. 11: 5-17.)

Nephi asked. The Lord answered the request. But he always left it to the Lord whether the request would be granted or denied. Nephi never demanded anything of the Lord. He meekly made requests and left it to the Lord.

In a recent example of the same kind of use of this power, President Thomas S. Monson described the dedicatory services at the new Temple in Brazil:

The evening before each of the temple dedications took place, magnificent cultural events were held. In Curitiba, Brazil, 4,330 members from the temple district, supported by a choir of 1,700 voices, presented a most inspirational program through song, dance, and video. The enormous soccer stadium where the event took place was filled with spectators. The wind had been blowing, and rain threatened. I offered a silent prayer asking Heavenly Father to look with mercy upon those who had prepared so diligently for our entertainment and whose costumes and presentations would be damaged if a heavy rain or wind enveloped them. He honored that prayer, and it wasn't until the end of the show and later on that evening that rain fell in abundance. (Monson, Thomas, S. *Welcome to Conference.* Ensign CR, October, 2008.)

Again, one holding sealing power "asked" for God "to look with mercy" on others. God "honored that prayer." The authority was used in a petition for others. President Monson had charity for those whose efforts were threatened by the weather. There was no demand, no insistence in the query; just a meek request.

If you go back and re-read the statements when sealing authority is openly conferred in the record of scripture, you will find that those who receive it are always meek. They will only use it under the Lord's direction and with the Lord's approval. In the case of Joseph Smith, read again Section 132, verse 46. Joseph is told by the Lord he will use the authority "by my word." Meaning it is the Lord's will and not Joseph's which is to be bound using this authority.

In the case of Nephi, he was identified by the Lord as someone who "shall not ask that which is contrary to my will." (Hel. 10: 5.) In the case of Alma, as Amulek asked that power be used to prevent the burning deaths of innocent women and children, Alma replied: "But Alma said unto him: *The Spirit constraineth me that I must not stretch forth mine hand*; for behold the Lord receiveth them up unto himself, in glory; and he doth suffer that they may do this thing, or that the people may do this thing unto them, according to the hardness of their hearts, that the judgments which he shall exercise upon them in his wrath may be just; and the blood of the innocent shall stand as a witness against them, yea, and cry mightily against them at the last day." (Alma 14: 11, emphasis added.)

The power to seal is tied to meekness. It is only through

meekness this authority can be given or exercised. Therefore, those who receive it and have the power to exercise it can only do so in conformity with the pattern of heaven. They must do as Christ did, or they have no right to seal. As modern revelation describes the process of conforming to God's will: "And, behold, and lo, this is an ensample unto all those who were ordained unto this priesthood, whose mission is appointed unto them to go forth-- And this is the ensample unto them, that they shall speak as they are moved upon by the Holy Ghost. And whatsoever they shall speak when moved upon by the Holy Ghost shall be scripture, shall be the will of the Lord, shall be the mind of the Lord, shall be the word of the Lord, shall be the voice of the Lord, and the power of God unto salvation." (D&C 68: 2-4.) To speak words which will seal on earth and in heaven requires a person to speak the words given to them by God. Whenever any person speaks the words of God as moved upon by His Holy Spirit, the words they speak **are** scripture. These words are the mind of the Lord. They are the will of the Lord. They are the power of God unto salvation.

In another statement to the same effect we read: "What I the Lord have spoken, I have spoken, and I excuse not myself; and though the heavens and the earth pass away, *my word shall not pass away, but shall all be fulfilled, whether by mine own voice or by the voice of my servants, it is the same.*" (D&C 1: 38, emphasis added.) This is applicable to the sealing power because anytime any person speaks the words given them from God, they shall all be fulfilled.

There is no magic in the sealing authority. It is a doctrine which ties authority to the power of heaven. This power is always ineffective if it is not used in conformity with the will of God. Read again how the sealing authority, or any priesthood authority, can *only* be used: "That the rights of the priesthood are *inseparably connected with the powers of heaven*, and that the *powers of heaven cannot be controlled nor handled only upon the principles of righteousness.* That they may be conferred upon us, it is true; but when we undertake to cover our sins, or to gratify our pride, our vain ambition, or to exercise control or dominion or compulsion upon the souls of the children of men, in any degree of unrighteousness, behold, *the heavens withdraw themselves*; the Spirit of the Lord is grieved; and *when it is withdrawn, Amen to the priesthood or the authority of that man.*" (D&C 121: 36-37, emphasis added.) Authority from God can only be successfully used in conformity with the will of God. The inverse is also true: **Anyone** who speaks in conformity with the will of God has the authority to bind. It is not the person who binds. It is the voice of God which does so. So the real question in every case is whether or not the person is speaking words which conform to God's will. No matter the office, no matter what has been conferred upon a person, no matter the credentials, family, position, rank or background, words which fail to mirror God's will fall to the ground unfulfilled. Amen to any authority which is contrary to God's command.

The only people who ever exercise sealing authority are those who do so at the direction of the Lord. They are necessarily meek. For it is only the meek who are given direction from the Lord.

Others may feign authority, gratify their pride and exercise control, they may put their vain ambition on display, but they will never seal a single thing in this life or the life to come.

The meekness required to control the elements and command the armies of heaven is best exemplified by Christ. He reminded Peter when Peter tried to prevent His arrest: "Thinkest thou that I cannot now pray to my Father, and he shall presently give me more than twelve legions of angels?" (Matt. 26: 53.) When He was brought before Pilate the record informs us: "The Jews answered him, We have a law, and by our law he ought to die, because he made himself the Son of God. When Pilate therefore heard that saying, he was the more afraid; And went again into the judgment hall, and saith unto Jesus, Whence art thou? But Jesus gave him no answer. Then saith Pilate unto him, Speakest thou not unto me? knowest thou not that I have power to crucify thee, and have power to release thee? *Jesus answered, Thou couldest have no power at all against me, except it were given thee from above.*" (John 19: 7-11.) Pilate's role was limited. The role delegated to him did not include the power over life and death of a God. Christ, the Son of God, the Almighty, Jehovah, Wonderful, Counselor, the Prince of Peace could have avoided death. But He pressed meekly on, refusing to call down twelve legions of angels. Refusing to command the wind and the waves which would obey His voice. He pressed forward in meekness to acquire also the titles of Lamb of God, Redeemer, Savior, and Resurrected Lord. He could then ask us all: "Therefore, what manner of men ought ye to be?" and answer His own inquiry:

"Verily I say unto you, even as I am." (3 Ne. 27: 27.)

The sealing authority is an essential part of having one's calling and election made sure. However, that authority as it turns out cannot be exercised in any manner other than the very way in which Christ exercised it. Only the meek will ever hold the power to bind on earth and in heaven. Because only the meek will submit to the Lord's will so completely as to be invited to speak under the guidance of the Holy Spirit words of eternal life. Remember the discussion at the beginning of this book about "intelligence" or the "light of truth" which is "the glory of God." Those who hold this power cannot exercise it contrary to the power of God. They know this. In the case of Enos, his own grandson was "a wicked man" who did not keep "the statutes and commandments of the Lord as [he] ought to have done." (Omni 1: 2.) There is no indication Enos used the sealing power he posssessed to secure this wayward grandson the promise of eternal life. Truly, the powers of heaven cannot be handled apart from the principles of righteousness.

It is little wonder that we will be judged by our "words" (see Alma 12: 14) because only the words we speak or write which are sealed to us will accompany any of us into the afterlife. We ought to exercise a good deal of prayerful caution in how we speak. We ought to speak in the Lord's name the words of eternal life. Unfortunately, many pretended Saints instead speak idle words, gratifying their pride, exercising their vain ambition, while using the Lord's name only in vain. Whenever someone proclaims their own agenda in the name of the Lord they take His name in vain. It is not swearing, but rather when one claims to speak for the Lord when they do not, that violates the command against vainly using the Lord's name.

Chapter 13

CONCLUSION

This is a world filled with change and decay. All things here are touched by entropy. Even truth dissipates unless it is continually renewed by effort. All of this is inevitable because decay is a product of the Fall of mankind and inherent with mortality. As a result of this natural state of decay, Latter-day Saints must guard the truths we possess or they will vanish. All past dispensations of the Gospel have decayed, finally resulting in apostasy. Without vigilance and great care, we can meet the same fate.

Latter-day Saint scholars increasingly claim they have the right to define truth. This is because scholars conflict with all other sources claiming to possess truth. But the faith delivered to us through Joseph Smith did not require scholarship to understand. It was necessarily simple. No matter how profound the truths are which came through Joseph, they remain simple. Scholars have a way of changing truth by applying sophisticated arguments because their stock in trade is to make things difficult. Unless they are able to sell their sophisticated vocabulary and talk down to the unwashed and uninitiated in their brand of mysteries, no one will hire them.

Our very best Latter-day Saint scholar was entirely contrite about the limits of scholarship. It was not a false faith for him. But he repeatedly raised the alarm about the competition between the role of scholars and the role of prophets. Hugh Nibley's recently published Volume 17 of his Collected Works includes this observation: "[W]hen the Church lost revelation it had to turn to another source for guidance and so threw itself into the arms of the established schools of learning. The schoolmen, as one of them expresses it, took over the office and function once belonging to the prophets and once in power guarded their authority with jealous care, quickly and violently suppressing any suggestion of a recurrent inspiration. ...By its very nature the university is the rival of the Church; its historic mission has been to supply the guiding light which passed away with the loss of revelation, and it can make no concessions to its absolute authority without forfeiting that authority." (Nibley Hugh, *Eloquent Witness: Nibley on Himself, Others and the Temple.* Salt Lake City: Deseret Book, 2008, p. 127.) Latter-day Saints would be foolish not to believe this conflict has already emerged inside our own faith.

We face an increasing and deliberate attempt to make the faith of the Latter-day Saints look, sound and read like mainstream Christianity. Opinion leaders believe we need to be accepted. Our faith came, however, because Heaven was revolted at mainstream Christianity, whose creeds were and are abominable and whose professors remain corrupt and unredeemed. The faith which was restored through Joseph differs markedly from what existed and still exists under the broad banner of Historic Christianity. There are limited similarities between the two. We should be criticized by them, because we are so very unlike them. At least we *ought* to be unlike them if we are interested in escaping the condemnation Christ leveled at them. In turn, we cannot give Historic Christianity unmitigated praise. Their doctrines are unacceptable to us. Any attempt to lessen the significant differences between the doctrines they believe and preach, and the ones we believe and preach can only come from us converting them. It cannot come by us downplaying or diminishing the differences.

I write to try and preserve a coherent statement of the faith which was returned to us. I do not write as a scholar and entertain no ambition to join with them. The simple truths of the Gospel may compete with scholarship, but it can never fully embrace it.

The Church of Jesus Christ of Latter-day Saints is the authorized repository of the keys to perform authoritative ordinances. It is also the institution through which tithes are collected and programs are organized. It is at present a multi-billion dollar enterprise with heavy administrative burdens to carry. We expect the Church to build meetinghouses, Temples and other necessary facilities such as Bishop's Storehouses. We also expect the Church will provide lesson materials, training manuals and teaching aids in all the languages of the world. We further expect the Church to continually organize and supervise Wards, Stakes, Missions, Districts and Areas throughout the entire world into separate divisions in which each is provided with ministering officers. We have weekly meetings, quarterly meetings, semi-annual meetings and annual meetings all organized and conducted through the Church. With respect to these expected duties the Church not only meets our expectations, it exceeds what we can reasonably expect.

With more than half of the Church comprised of first-generation converts, we cannot expect it to instruct all its members in the fullness of all its doctrine and mysteries. Indeed, most mysteries are **supposed** to be learned in self-pursuit by the individual. This book is intended as an aid for those in self-pursuit of the things restored through Joseph using Enos as an example of ultimate success.

Even if you comprehend all mysteries, you are of little use to God and your fellowman unless you minister to the sick, feed the hungry, clothe the naked, visit the confined, and give relief to the needy. Paul was right in that knowledge of mysteries pales in comparison to charity toward others. Even if you understand all the Book of Mormon teaches, if you fail to have charity toward others, your knowledge is of little value to you or to others.

We have been using Enos' record to examine a path or pattern. The pattern is in the scriptures to guide our own lives. If we only see in this account one man's unique experience in becoming acquainted with God, I have failed to make the most important point. The record is the pattern. It is written to advise **you** in your life. **You** must become acquainted with God. Unless you do, you will fail. Promises obtained by others through faith can never benefit you. You must go and do likewise for this process to have any relevance in your life. Enos became acquainted with God because he had compassion for his fellow man. He prayed for his "brethren" the Lamanites whose "hatred was fixed" toward the Nephites. He made intercession for them. This is the pattern for us all.

Joseph Smith is not on trial. The Book of Mormon is not on trial. You are. The only limits God imposes upon you is that you must follow the path He has marked out, and which His Son demonstrated with perfection. If you follow in that path you will develop faith. Once that faith has matured, been tested and tried, it will become a source of power and light for you. There are no exceptions. The plan and its requirements are universal.

Enos is the most interesting writer in the Book of Mormon. He is the favorite of many Latter-day Saints. Hopefully this book about Enos' record will make him the favorite of many more. His discipleship approached perfection itself. His brief record etched on the dwindling space available on the Small Plates of Nephi shows the brilliant mind of an adept writer who mastered the use of symbols. Enos presumes the meaning of his symbolic language will elude readers who are unprepared to see it. But every Latter-day Saint ought to be able to read and understand this prophet. He defines for each of us how we can gain eternal life.

Another thought about how to follow Enos' example: When Enos raised his voice high, to heaven, it had nothing to do with volume. It had to do with the quality of the communication, the content of his soul as he sought further light and knowledge. There should be moments in every life when you put aside all the distractions, worries and troubles of this world and you ponder deeply about God. It is only in such quiet, still moments when our minds can reach into heaven itself. We can feel things long before we are able to see them. When prophets who have written scripture get into the quiet, calm frame of mind which allows them to feel the things of God, they often use the word "ponder" to describe how they prepared. It is a good word. It describes in a single word the still moments when you put aside the cares of the world and approach God with solemn and careful thoughts. There are no "words" really spoken at such moments. Rather we are just open to receive. We are willing to allow God within us. We flee from the cares of Babylon and go to a state where the still, the calm, the penetrating voice of God can finally be heard.

Those who let these moments wash over them are called prophets and prophetesses. They can feel what is coming before it happens. They know the signs of the times because heaven is opened to them. We were all intended to be such people. Enos is just one example of how those who follow Christ are led inevitably to do as Christ did. When cares pressed upon Him, Christ "departed thence by ship into a desert place apart." (Matt 14: 13.) To allow His Apostles to drink in that same still, quiet mind which alone allowed them to ponder deeply, He "said unto them, Come ye yourselves apart into a desert place, and rest a while: for there were many coming and going, and they had no leisure so much as to eat." (Mark 6: 31.) After teaching a gathering, it is written: "And when he had sent the multitudes away, he went up into a mountain apart to pray: and when the evening was come, he was there alone." (Matt. 14: 23.) And again: "When Jesus therefore perceived that they would come and take him by force, to make him a king, he departed again into a mountain himself alone." (John 6: 15.) You need to realize that spiritual enlightenment is not something which you are going to achieve or accomplish. You are not going to attain, earn or acquire spiritual blessings. You will receive them - if you receive them at all - by being open to God's gifts. He gives freely. But unless we are quiet enough, open enough, and prayerful enough to be apart, to be alone, to be in solemn, careful and ponderous thought, we will never receive what is freely given to all. Joseph's formula remains the best: "[T]he things of God are of deep import; and time, and experience, and careful and ponderous and solemn thoughts can only find them out. Thy mind, O man! if thou wilt lead a soul unto salvation, must stretch as high as the utmost heavens, and search into and contemplate the darkest abyss, and the broad expanse of eternity-thou must commune with God. How much more dignified and noble are the thoughts of God, than the vain imaginations of the human heart!" (*TPJS*, p. 137.) Paul put it this way: "study to be quiet." (1 Thes. 4: 11.) Modern revelation captures this experience with these words: "Yea, thus saith the still small voice, which whispereth through and pierceth all things, and often times it maketh my bones to quake while it maketh manifest." (D&C 85: 6.)

Enos' voice rose high into the heavens. His voice could only go there by using the calm still power of the Spirit. God's voice to the Nephites is given this description: "it was not a harsh voice, neither was it a loud voice; nevertheless, and notwithstanding it being a small voice it did pierce them that did hear to the center, insomuch that there was no part of their frame that it did not cause to quake; yea, it did pierce them to the very soul, and did cause their hearts to burn." (3 Ne. 11: 3.) The voice of the Spirit, the voice of God comes as a small, penetrating and powerful statement which cuts to the very center of your being. When your own thoughts are small and pure, they also can penetrate to the place where God resides. You must use the same medium to speak to Him as He uses to speak to you. Study to be calm. For only then will you be like Enos and proclaim: "I did still raise my voice high that it reached the heavens." (Verse 4.)

A final important thought: just like former dispensations of the Gospel, truths can slip away from us if we do not labor to preserve them. I have discussed the Book of Enos with an interpretive eye toward preserving important doctrine. However important doctrine may be, you should always remember it is not the most important component of the Gospel of Jesus Christ. The Apostle Paul reminded us that understanding mysteries and possessing knowledge alone will not save anyone. He wrote: "And though I have the gift of prophecy, and understand all mysteries, and all knowledge; and though I have all faith, so that I could remove mountains, and have not charity, I am nothing." (1 Cor. 13: 2.)

Enos concerned himself with the welfare of others at the very moment when he was in closest contact with the Lord. His petition for God's blessing went out on behalf of his enemies as well as his brethren. I am concerned that some may think understanding the doctrine is the same thing as having favor with God. Without charity toward your fellow man - and not just your family, friends and those who are like you, but also toward those who are so very unlike you that they become your enemies - without charity toward them, your understanding is of no real benefit. Quite the contrary, a great understanding of the deepest doctrines may condemn you all the more.

It is the conduct of Enos which matters most. His love of others, including us, is better to copy in your life than to merely become a point for discussion. It is one thing to understand his record and testimony and another to follow his example. As with Enos, your conduct matters the most. If this book distracts from understanding that point then it has done a disservice. As this book concludes, let me reiterate again Enos' most important message is to be found in his charity toward others. His intimate relationship with the Lord was derived from that. If you want to know the Lord, then turn your search into serving your fellow man. The more you love your fellow man the closer you draw to their Redeemer.

THE END

BIBLIOGRAPHY

Backman, Milton V., Jr. *Joseph Smith's First Vision*. Second Edition. Salt Lake City: Bookcraft, 1971.

Buerger, David John. *The Mysteries of Godliness*. San Francisco: Smith Research Associates, 1994.

Hinkley, Gordon B. *God Is at the Helm*. Ensign CR, May, 1994.

History of the Church of Jesus Christ of Latter-day Saints, 7 Volumes, published by the Church of Jesus Christ of Latter-day Saints.

Lectures on Faith, compiled by N.B. Lundwall, published by Bookcraft.

McConkie, Bruce R. *Doctrinal New Testament Commentary, Vol. 3, Colossians - Revelation*. Salt Lake City: Bookcraft, 1973.

McConkie, Bruce R. *The Ten Blessings of the Priesthood*. Ensign CR, November, 1977.

Monson, Thomas, S. *Welcome to Conference*. Ensign CR, October, 2008.

Nibley Hugh, *Eloquent Witness: Nibley on Himself, Others and the Temple*. Salt Lake City: Deseret Book, 2008.

Packer, Boyd K. *Covenants*. Ensign CR, May, 1987.

Packer, Boyd K. *On Zion's Hill*. Ensign CR October, 2005.

Romney, Marion G. *The Light of Christ*. Ensign CR, May, 1977.

Smith, Joseph Fielding. *Doctrines of Salvation*. Edited by Bruce R. McConkie. 3 volumes. Salt Lake City: Bookcraft, 1956.

Smith, Joseph Fielding. *Answers to Gospel Questions, Volume 4. 5 Volumes*. Salt Lake City: Deseret Book, 1963.

Snuffer, Denver C., Jr. *The Second Comforter: Conversing With the Lord Through the Veil*. Second Edition. Salt Lake City. Mill Creek Press, 2008.

Sorenson, John L. *Religious Groups and Movements Among the Nephites, 200-1B.C.* found in *The Disciple as Scholar: Essays on Scripture and the Ancient World in Honor of Richard Lloyd Anderson*. Edited by Steven D. Ricks, Donald W. Parry, and Andrew H. Hedges. Provo: FARMS, 2000.

Teachings of the Prophet Joseph Smith. Arranged by Joseph Fielding Smith. Salt Lake City: Deseret Book Company, 1972.

Vesilind, Priit, J. Watery Graves of the Maya. *National Geographic*, October 2003.

The Worlds of Joseph Smith. Edited by John W. Welch. Provo: Brigham Young University Press, 2006.

INDEX

About the Author

DENVER C. SNUFFER, JR. is an attorney living in Sandy, Utah. He has an Associates of Arts degree from Daniel Webster Jr. College, Bachelors of Business Administration from McMurry University, and Juris Doctor from the J. Reuben Clark Law School at Brigham Young University. He was admitted to practice law in 1980 in Utah, and has been a practicing attorney since then. A convert to the LDS faith in 1973 when 19 years old, he has now been a member of the LDS Church for over thirty-three years. Recently released from serving on the Sandy Crescent Stake High Council, he served on the Draper Temple Open House Committee before returning to serve in the Young Men's program in his home ward. Previously he has taught Gospel Doctrine and Priesthood classes for twenty-one years in Wards in Pleasant Grove, Alpine and Sandy, Utah. He has instructed Graduate Institute classes at the University of Utah College of Law for two years, and instructed at the BYU Education Week for three years. After a decade, he recently concluded teaching a weekly class on the Book of Mormon. He is the author of four other books, *The Second Comforter: Conversing With the Lord Through the Veil*, published by Mill Creek Press in 2006, second edition in 2008, *Nephi's Isaiah*, published by Mill Creek Press in 2006, *Eighteen Verses*, published by Mill Creek Press in 2007, and *Ten Parables*, published by Mill Creek Press in 2008.

A Note On The Type

This book was set in Garamond. The fonts are based on the fonts first cut by Claude Garamond (c. 1480-1561). Garamond was a pupil of Geoffroy Tory and is believed to have followed the Venetian models, although he introduced a number of important differences, and it is to him that we owe the letter we now know as "old style." He gave to his letters a certain elegance and feeling of movement that won their creator an immediate reputation and the patronage of Francis I of France.

Designed by Mill Creek Press

Cover by Michael S. Eldredge, Jr.
Salt Lake City, Utah

Printed and bound by BookSurge Publishing,
Charleston, South Carolina

www.ingramcontent.com/pod-product-compliance
Lightning Source LLC
Chambersburg PA
CBHW030927090426
42737CB00007B/341